MIND:
YOUR
CONSCIOUSNESS
IS
WHAT
AND
WHERE?

MIND

YOUR CONSCIOUSNESS IS WHAT AND WHERE?

TED HONDERICH

REAKTION BOOKS LTD

To Ingrid, Pauline, Jane, John Ruan, Kiaran, Renet,
John Allen, Mary, David, Birgit

Published by

REAKTION BOOKS LTD
Unit 32, Waterside
44–48 Wharf Road
London N1 7UX, UK
www.reaktionbooks.co.uk

First published 2017
Copyright © Ted Honderich 2017

All rights reserved

No part of this publication may be reproduced, stored in a retrieval system,
or transmitted, in any form or by any means, electronic, mechanical,
photocopying, recording or otherwise, without the prior permission
of the publishers

Printed and bound in Great Britain
by TJ International, Padstow, Cornwall

A catalogue record for this book is available from the British Library

ISBN 978 1 78023 821 0

CONTENTS

INVITATION TO READERS

Your mind, your consciousness right now, what you perhaps call your *existing*, what some call your spirit – the questions of what they are, what they come to, are paralysing or anyway numbing; maybe as much so today as they were in the seventeenth century when the great French philosopher René Descartes announced that most famous proof in all philosophy, 'I think, therefore I am.'

Those questions about each of us, and possibly of computers that are to come, are stuff of the philosophy of mind, psychology and neuroscience, and such travelling companions as linguistics, psychiatry, psychoanalysis, a society's law, courts and religion, and the Mind and Spirit shelf of a bookshop. They are as asked and answered and disagreed about as questions can be. One neuroscientist and philosopher is known just for naming the consciousness question, or part of it, 'the hard problem'. He meant that it is a lot harder than what you can call 'the brain problem'.

Philosophy, you can hear, despite an old definition of it as love of wisdom, is neither wise nor deep, nor wonderfully loving, but rather concentration on the logic of perfectly ordinary intelligence – rather than science's concentration on facts. Certainly it does not own the subject or subjects of mind, consciousness, existing and spirit, but it goes on as if it can claim first right to them.

More people than philosophers and scientists of mind remember the name of Descartes mainly for his dualism, although he was certainly preceded by some ancient Greeks. The idea, conviction or doctrine is that mind and brain are in some important way two things, not one thing. Mind is different from brain in being spirit, soul, *pneuma* or 'breath' as distinct from body. As distinct, it seems, from anything whatsoever that is just physical.

On the other hand, more people than philosophers and scientists of mind are more than tempted by two ideas. One is the idea or anyway the word that consciousness is *real* – their own consciousness is more real to them than anything else. And isn't what is real what is physical? Isn't that what any clear reality is? So what has been called monism rather than dualism is the idea that everything is physical.

You may be more impressed by something else not at all vague. Whatever else is true of your consciousness, it surely has physical effects. It has the effect of this page's being open in front of you right now. And how could anything that has physical effects not be physical itself? That would be a pretty fantastic idea, wouldn't it? It would go against the whole history of science, wouldn't it?

That is just a start on the rich history and present active carry-on of philosophy, neuroscience and the rest about mind, and in particular what seems unique to it – consciousness.

Within dualism and monism there are very many *theories* of consciousness. That is to say that there are very many different answers to the question of what it comes to, what its nature is. That has to somehow be the first question, before the question of how consciousness or mind is related to brain – even if some people jump to the conclusion that somehow consciousness or mind *is* brain.

Some recent theories boil down to some version, sometimes a very surprising one, of the idea that consciousness does indeed have effects. Or, better, a conscious event or state, we are told, is *just* something in causal connections with what preceded it and what followed it. In a particular and indeed unusual use of the word, a conscious state is something that has a certain *function*.

Maybe that can sound OK, but what if in addition we say that what has the function is or somehow includes or involves what is *abstract*? You can get to that idea, whatever it is, by way of what is a truth, idea or impulse. Can't it be that two different physical things, maybe you and a very up-to-date computer or a computer to come, can have one and same idea, maybe intention? Isn't there something you can call the *multiple realizability* of just one thought or feeling? Maybe, in passing, of 2 + 2 = 4? Something not just general but also abstract?

That is just one of at least half a dozen theories; there are very many more if you make more distinctions between theories. There are neuroscientists who are at least tempted to panpsychism or to what Bertrand Russell called neutral monism or the like, which are all somehow along the line that *everything* is both physical and mental. There are also thinkers beginning from the fact of language who somehow explain consciousness in terms of representation or aboutness. There is my own old thing, now dead as a doornail, called the union theory, that a thought and a brain event are somehow one single effect.

It wasn't absurd for a good philosopher to say that we humans have no more chance of solving the consciousness question than chimpanzees have of doing quantum theory. Still, there are lots of other things that we can be baffled by. Perhaps we might include the nature of truth or of what is right. But a question has arisen in a mind or two. Can it be that there has been all that disagreement about what consciousness is as a result of people not asking a clear question, or not agreeing on a question?

You may have heard enough already to wonder about that. In fact, if we look at leading first ideas or identifications of the subject of consciousness, leading formulations of the question of what it is or comes to, it seems to me, and it may seem to you, that we do not get a decent start in one clear question.

But there is one. It takes some bravery to get there – because Noam Chomsky, the saviour of the science of linguistics and a man otherwise unique in our societies, has declared that the history of science, particularly physics, stands in the way of any clear question about consciousness and physicality. But I still think we can get there.

Like so much in the history of science rather than philosophy, so many first moves towards theories or understandings, the start we can make is figurative or metaphorical. But, by way of other reflection and argument – a lot of it about the whole subject of physicality itself, starting with objective physicality, and a lot of it about three whole sides of consciousness, perceptual, cognitive and affective – the start can eventually issue a fully literal rather than figurative or metaphorical theory.

It can lead to a unique theory whose setting out in this book is a culmination of the stages of my struggle in thinking about consciousness. The theory really is something very different, which philosophers and scientists have certainly kept saying we need.

Does this philosophical theory help with the science of consciousness? Is it a theory that has such further recommendations as fertility – giving rise to more new work, say, about all perceiving, including seeing the room you're in in particular? Does it make sense of the thing or things we call subjectivity, by seeing subjectivity partly in terms of what has been the separate and plainer question of personal identity – *who* you are? Does the theory help, surprisingly, with the ancient question of determinism and freedom? Can the theory itself show that we picked the right subject of consciousness, asked the right question?

Above all, will *you* recognize it as pretty clear truth, or in any case on the way to it, truth as to *your* being conscious right now? Is there a subject in philosophy or anything else that you are better placed to judge? You've got data.

ACTUALISM ANTICIPATED

The theory of consciousness of this book, Actualism, is a long way from what are to me two big fairy tales still being told and elaborated in various ways in response to the greatest problem in the philosophy and science of mind: the problem of what our being conscious is.

One fairy tale is that all consciousness really is just objective, scientific or standard physical stuff in your head, soggy grey matter, as some say – or meat. As many others say more piously, consciousness is wondrously complex but still only *neural* networks, networks of cells. In both cases it is fundamentally the same kind of thing as the chair you're sitting on, despite the differences. The other fairy tale is that all consciousness is immaterial or ghostly stuff. That is the old, old theory of mind–brain *dualism*, mind and brain being two different things, but also a theory newish in both philosophy and in cognitive science.

The newish thing in this age of the computer is the theory of *abstract functionalism*. Consciousness is events or states, 'an abstract sort of thing', happening somehow unphysically *above* brains, related to the brain stuff below that is connected somehow functionally or causally with other physical events or states, maybe with consciousness above them too. But, as I and maybe you are tempted to say, with the consciousness anywhere existing only in thought.

To try to do better, in what follows we'll start by looking at some differences.

There's your being conscious right now in seeing the room or the other place you're in. You're also thinking something right now as a result of this very sentence. Thirdly, you're probably feeling something, maybe hope. Your consciousness in general, consciousness in the primary ordinary sense, the core sense, the one in decent dictionaries, has those three different sides.

So there's perceptual consciousness *within* seeing and other perception – perceiving as a whole, of course, comes to more than consciousness, such as facts about eyes. And there's cognitive consciousness, which we can also label as thinking. And affective consciousness, which we can label as wanting and the like.

There will be the general question of what all consciousness is, what it comes to, what the three sides have in common. There will also be the three particular questions of what each of the sides of consciousness comes to – to which a first answer will be that they certainly are not the three mysterious old medieval *faculties* or *powers* of the mind, which were more or other than ordinary consciousness.

Those four are the main questions, but there will be others, which of course are connected. One is that of the relation between your being conscious in general and your brain, your neural processes. That relation is probably the main subject in science of mind, usually in the past called the mind–body problem, to which both objective physicalism and dualism are answers as well as being answers to what consciousness is. That isn't all the large matter of what all of *the mind* is, including all the mental processes past and present that issue in consciousness, but it's not far off.

There will also be the question that you may think is easily answered – the question of *where* your consciousness is. It's got to be *somewhere*, doesn't it? In your head? Behind your forehead? Some philosophers have modified that intuitive answer of internalism or cranialism a little.

Modified it nearly enough?

And there will be that further question about each of us – about what is still called a *self*. What is one of those? The great philosopher David Hume had a look into himself and couldn't find his at all. But consciousness does involves a connected fact of what is called *subjectivity*, doesn't it? Philosophers and scientists have gone on about that a lot.

There is no agreement in philosophy or science or anywhere else about the answer to the general question of what or where consciousness is or the questions about its three sides or sorts, or the secondary questions. The ongoing disagreement has resulted in a wide pessimism about our solving the general problem of consciousness. The resolute philosopher Colin McGinn was known in the past for saying that we have no more chance of solving the consciousness problem than chimps have of doing quantum theory. He has since at least modified what was called his mysterianism quite a lot, but not become an optimist. He certainly is not alone in his pessimism.

If you spend some time looking into the competing general theories of consciousness, including the two great fairy tales and a lot of other theories and also various impulses and ideas (see the bibliographies at the end of this book for relevant books and articles), a question may come to your mind and stay there. Is there all this disagreement mainly or partly because the theorists are just not talking about the same thing? Is the disagreement or maybe mainly just *seeming* disagreement about consciousness owed to people just thinking about different things, meaning different subjects by the word 'consciousness'? Not asking and answering the same question? It's known elsewhere in life: say, in politics. More fundamentally, has there not been what we can call *an adequate initial clarification* of the subject of *ordinary* consciousness in our philosophy and science? Is it the case, for a good start, that there is no such thing as this in the five leading ideas of the philosophy and science of consciousness? Is there an adequate initial clarification in the first idea, which is to the effect that consciousness is somehow a matter of your having *qualia*? These items are said variously to be the ways things seem, or features of mental states, or experiential properties of sensations, or feelings, perceptions, wants or emotions. Or somehow similar properties of thinking itself somehow conceived, maybe even of what we are inclined to call purely logical or factual thoughts.

Sometimes qualia are taken to include or be those personal and of course internal properties in our seeing and hearing and so on that in past centuries used to be called *ideas* in a special sense, or *impressions*.

The philosopher Daniel Dennett, a rightly renowned physicalist, says qualia are *the ways things seem to us*, the particular personal, subjective qualities of experience at the moment. The independent philosopher Thomas Nagel, also American, says qualia are features of *mental* states – presumably he means conscious states. Very unlike Dennett, he says it seems impossible to analyse them in objective physical terms, make sense of them as objectively physical – whatever it is for anything to be that.

Ned Block, philosopher-psychologist, has it that qualia include not only *experiential* properties of sensations, feelings, perceptions, wants and emotions, but such experiential properties of *thoughts*, what we can call pure thoughts, anyway our thoughts that are different from what is taken to be just the functioning of unconscious computers – just computation or bare computation.

John Searle of California, a severe and persuasive judge of some science of consciousness, says of qualia as he understands them, maybe acutely, that consciousness right down to the ground, *all* of consciousness, is just qualia. His point, presumably, is in fact that the character or some character assigned to qualia is something had by *all* of consciousness, every last fact of it.

Well then, taking into account all these views, we won't get a first clarification of consciousness with qualia – because of the disagreement and uncertainty about the things. But, even more fatally, we also won't get a clarification since it's agreed from the start by almost all or most of the enthusiasts who have been called qualia freaks that there is *more* to consciousness than qualia. There's something else already touched on. That is the part of consciousness you can call pure thinking, sometimes called *propositional attitudes*, just thoughts, usually supposed to be without qualia. This very sentence, like any sentence here, expresses one.

You can't begin to have a clarification of a subject that leaves out half of it. That's not quite all. There's the further fact that qualia are given to us as *qualities of* consciousness, not what *has* the qualities, not consciousness itself. That's what we want to know about, isn't it? Anyway we want something like all the qualities.

A second leading idea in the philosophy and science of consciousness is owed to Nagel, in particular to his very well-known paper 'What is It Like to Be a Bat?' What the idea comes to is that what it is for something to be conscious, say what it is for a bat or for you to be conscious, is for there to be *something it is like to be that thing*.

One objection to or difficulty with this idea is first that in a clear sense of the words there is something it is like to be *anything*. There is something it is like to be this page or indeed a chair or any other unconscious thing. It is for the thing to have certain properties. That can lead you to the good idea that what is being offered to us in this second idea of consciousness is just the special proposition that what it is for a thing to be conscious is there being *what it is like for the thing to be conscious*. This is circularity, the very thing supposed to be defined or explained in fact occurring undefined or explained in the supposed definition or explanation.

The third idea is that of subjectivity, already mentioned. In recent philosophy of mind, it is in fact some number of ideas, of which what it is tempting to call the primitive one was of *a self* or *a subject* or *homunculus* within each of us. A thing in the thing, maybe a kind of owner. It was indeed a contribution to philosophy of Hume, if not his largest contribution, to record that he had no awareness in being conscious of such an internal entity.

The fourth leading idea is what on account of a precedent in medieval philosophy has traditionally been called *intentionality* – and is now better called just *aboutness*. Who can say that our subject of consciousness does not include *something* that is aboutness? That is not to think, despite the reflectively resolute Tim Crane of Cambridge, that talk of aboutness can by itself identify all consciousness for us. If aboutness is thought of as the general property of something's representing something else, in some such way as a name represents a person, is *all* of consciousness representative?

It has usually been supposed by philosophers that aboutness when clearly and explicitly enough understood is evidently a property of, say, beliefs, but is not a property of, say, aches or maybe undirected depression. Aches are not *about* things in the sense that names are – even if they are causes of what are in fact about them, say, what you say of your ache.

The fifth leading idea will be that more recent one, *phenomenality*, associated primarily with Block. The idea is not easy to get hold of. Consciousness, or rather half of what he speaks of as consciousness, is a matter of this fact, which perhaps is to be identified as or by way of experiencing or sensing or directly apprehending. Well, if those are to give us an adequate initial clarification of consciousness, they will need to have more said of them – answers to what they are.

That is not all the problem. It is indeed put to us by Block that there are two kinds of consciousness: phenomenal consciousness and another kind, which second kind lacks precisely the character of phenomenal consciousness. Well then, there's no adequate initial clarification of consciousness in phenomenality.

So much for anticipation of the five leading ideas. And also of the bravery of David Chalmers, of both his native Australia and also New York, in running them all together in an understanding of consciousness – indeed regarding the central terms in or for the five of them, starting with 'qualia', as *synonyms*, about which claim you must have more than a doubt?

But that resistance of mine to the five ideas is not just dismissal. It definitely is not to say that certain items within the fuller expositions of the five ideas, things said in passing, will be of no use to us – in a larger and longer enterprise, getting to and putting together the theory of consciousness that is Actualism. Credit, then, to the makers and defenders of the five ideas.

The larger enterprise will begin from a certain big assortment of better convictions, inclinations or impulses about our being conscious – on all our parts. Are these better than than the five leading ideas? Yes, you will hear, we can and must begin from them. Begin from a kind of empiricism within philosophy. Begin from what it is right to call this *database*.

It is data from our personal holds on our consciousnesses, our immediately recalling pieces of them, which is not some funny nineteenth-century thing called introspection, inner peering, but data from a lot of others' and our own language, from books and from papers in journals – in short, a big collection of stuff. It is not just a philosopher's good guess on a Monday morning. Nor a scientist's gut feeling guiding research, however good.

Just some of about forty or fifty convictions, inclinations or impulses are that your being conscious right now in the ordinary sense, in any of the three ways, is:

something's being *had*,
something being *given*,
something being *present*,
something being *close*,
the *experiencing* of something,
something's being apparent or obvious,
something being what the good McGinn called vividly naked,
in the case of perception, there being the world as it is *for* something,
something being not deduced or inferred or posited or constructed from something else,
something being *to* or *for* something else,
something existing and known,
something itself somehow *real*,
something being *right there*,
something proximal, not distal.

These initial convictions and so on are largely metaphorical or figurative, like some or much or most of what is issued in the beginning in most science on everything. Something's being had or given in the senses used is not something's being had in the way of ankles or shoes, or given in the way of money. That the database is largely metaphorical or figurative, however, certainly does not entail that the theory or explanation of the nature of consciousness to which it may be an essential contribution will itself be anything less than perfectly literal.

Something's being actual is a summary or a label for what is conveyed of consciousness by the database. A summary or label for ordinary consciousness as being what we can call *actual consciousness*. So ordinary consciousness = something's being actual = actual consciousness.

Via the database itself we do have what we didn't get from the five leading ideas – *an adequate initial clarification* of ordinary consciousness. A *theory* or *analysis* or *account of the nature* of this consciousness, saying what this consciousness is, is indeed what the database and the labels eventually lead to. Saying literally and explicitly what this consciousness comes to: that's the job in hand.

We will move forward partly by way of this foundation and partly by way of something else. You've already heard two criteria for a successful theory of ordinary consciousness. It will have to explain *what* is actual with respect to this consciousness. It will also have to explain what this *being actual* is. There are more criteria. We get several from what were unkindly called those two big fairy tales, devout objective physicalism about consciousness and then dualism about consciousness and brain. They require attention, in my opinion, mainly for that reason of criteria.

The very short story from the two of them is that we will have to have a theory of consciousness that makes consciousness what we can call *real*, in particular something that can cause such physical events as where your arms and chairs are. And we have to have a theory that makes it *different* in kind from everything else, for a start different from the objective physical world, which of course dualism does.

There are more criteria to be had from thinking about a bundle of other more particular consciousness theories. The dependence or what is called the supervenience of consciousness on the brain, specific naturalisms or scientisms, special representationisms, computerism, double-aspect theories, panpsychism, my own old union theory, now abandoned, and what is called higher order theory, from David Rosenthal at CUNY, to the effect that being conscious is something's going on about which there is also something else higher but very similar going on simultaneously.

Getting more criteria will be our urgent reason for looking at these argued theories. One criterion is that a good theory will include a clear and good answer to the mind–body problem, the problem of the relation of consciousness to the brain.

We will move on from our adequate initial identification of the subject matter of ordinary consciousness and the subject of criteria. We can move towards a theory or understanding of what ordinary consciousness is, its nature – not by a leap straight from the database but first by way of a certain large subject whose consideration is prompted by both the database and the particular theories: the subject of the objective or scientific physical world and of objective physical things in general. We can get them straight not by theorizing but, so to speak, mainly by walking around in them.

As with consciousness and the database, this is another piece of empiricism within philosophy. Enough to help us try to stand up against the uniquely formidable free-thinker, indeed the great free-thinker, Noam Chomsky? Against his radical judgement that there exists *no* adequate conception of physicality, given what has happened within the history of science since the seventeenth century? What has happened since what you might call the age of simple particles? And hence that the question of the relation of consciousness to the physical is without clarity, sense, even coherence?

It turns out in our walking around that the objective physical world has sixteen characteristics. They start with objective physical things being those in the inventory of science – within what science generally takes to exist – and being open to the scientific method. But then also their being in or taking up space and time, being in lawful connections, standing in some connection or rather connections with perception, and so on.

Now we will come to a crunch, or rather crunches, to first large steps in the theory of consciousness. Two questions. Given that consciousness in its three parts is something, something or other, being actual, and physicality seems to be in the story somehow, *what* is it that is actual? And, secondly, what is that *being actual*?

The answers, which are indeed the main stuff of a theory of what consciousness is, an account of its nature, are different in the three cases; very different in the first case as against the second and third taken together.

Start with your consciousness itself right now *in* seeing and hearing, touching and so on, consciousness in any perceiving. What is actual is *a room or other thing out there*, whatever else needs to be said. There's only that one answer. Again, more generally, what is actual with your perceptual consciousness now, say with your seeing, is indeed a stage or part of what we will get around to calling *a subjective physical world*.

What is actual is not something or other *of* or *about* a room or a world, not an *image* or *idea* or what-not *of* something else. Not a representation or aboutness of any kind anywhere, of a room or other thing. What is actual is definitely not what used to be called or still is called a sense-datum, or a sign, symbol, picture, diagram, map, mental paint, content in a vague sense, or any other sort of representation or aboutness. What is actual is none of that past, present or maybe future stuff.

What is actual is in fact not anything in your head. What is actual just *is* a room.

And a room's *being actual*? That is *its somehow or other existing out there*, no more than that – its existing out there but not when you're not on hand. In my case when I go downstairs from this place up here. A room's existing out there when it is there but its not being the objective physical world. A shocking proposition? Well there have been shocks in philosophy before now. And more in science. Some became accepted, true – because they turned out to rest sufficiently on argument and fact.

A room's or a world's being actual, more particularly, is its being *subjectively physical* – being that kind of physical. Its having a lot of characteristics – also sixteen in number – related to but partly different from those of the objective physical world. That is what this being subjectively physical comes to. One of the worlds, yours, exists partly in that it is *lawfully dependent*, dependent as a matter of natural or scientific law or necessity, on something else out there – the *objective physical world*. And also being *lawfully dependent in this way on something else, you neurally*, on your brain and so on – just as dependent. This second dependency is what further identifies and distinguishes a subjective physical world.

So – being conscious in general, all of consciousness, isn't all of it an internal fact, just a cranial fact? That has always or as good as always been supposed by past theories of all of consciousness – despite the few recent smallish moves by Tyler Burge of Los

Angeles, Andy Clark of Edinburgh and Alva Noë of Berkeley towards what we can with large reason call our own externalism rather than internalism or cranialism. For us in our theory some of conciousness, perceptual consciousness, will really be just *an external fact*, anyway more external.

So much for perceptual consciousness. Now for cognitive and affective consciousness, kinds of thinking and wanting. There are several theories to be considered of various kinds, one having to do with what is called the language of thought – LOT – and also what we can call languages of thought, these being the assortment of ordinary thoughts. But the first main truth for us is that *what's* actual here *is* definitely aboutnesses of a kind. Cognitive aboutnesses have to do somehow with truth or not. Affective awarenesses have to do somehow with what is good or not. Both are things somehow, like the printed words in these very lines of type. Except they are not out there on the page or screen or on anything at all that is out there; they are internal to you or somebody else instead.

The second main truth is that the aboutnesses *being actual*, as in the case of subjective physical worlds, is also *their somehow existing*. But not in just the way of either those subjective worlds or of ordinary objectively or scientifically physical chairs. Your aboutnesses with thinking and wanting being actual also turn out to be their being *subjectively physical but differently so*, not only from the objective physical world but from your subjective physical world with perceptual consciousness. Different if counterpart characteristics, including place in both cases.

All this theory, *Actualism*, you will hear, satisfies the various criteria for a good theory of consciousness. For a start Actualism, unlike what we started with, objective physicalism, makes consciousness *different from everything else*. In fact it makes it strange, certainly unique. But that is what we have all thought and said it is; what in my view we can say that we know we know about it. And Actualism, unlike dualism and abstract functionalism, makes our consciousness what can indeed cause our arm movements and all the rest, including where chairs are.

Those are the main propositions to come in this book after this introduction – except for such other ones as those on the mind–body problem and on subjectivity as really an *individuality* as we will call it – or *personal identity*.

And there is also a sizeable proposition about aboutness in consciousness. The American philosopher Jerry Fodor is known for his despair about understanding this aboutness. He famously said that if aboutness is real it must be something else. Well, yes, it's different from aboutnesses not within consciousness – say these very sentences on paper. They will of course still be representations when nobody is reading them. Aboutnesses in consciousness will turn out to have the very different fact about them that they are *actual*.

There are also lesser propositions to come, one about the old but ongoing problem of *free will* as against determinism or what is better called explanationism. Another is about what is called naive realism, that in perceiving, we're in some kind of direct touch with what's out there – not with some image or other representation of it. Is Actualism the very different explicit and developed truth of that old philosophical chestnut?

There's also a proposition to come at the very end about whether we've been on about consciousness in the right sense in being on about ordinary or actual consciousness, to which the answer sensibly will be neither yes nor no. There is no one consciousness that is *the* right one. There is no consciousness into which we *must* inquire. There *is* a consciousness, ordinary or actual consciousness, which is unique in being essential to any other idea of consciousness, including the curious idea of consciousness as *all* of the mental, of which only a part is actual consciousness.

If you're impatient, if you still want to put the cart before the horse, want to get the whole cat a little more out of the bag right now – well, look right now at another summary, the final thing, but just a table of categories. Look at the comparative table on pp. 162–3 of the characteristics of physicality in general and then its kinds and hence the kinds that are consciousness.

So much for introductory summary or anticipation or route map of all of where we are going, all that follows.

As you'll have gathered, it will be philosophy – main-line philosophy. That's not mystery or deepness or the pursuit of wisdom or something confined to the English language or whatever. Even if there are kinds of it, including national kinds, and also Continental philosophy, it's just concentration on the logic of ordinary intelligence. Not pop philosophy, whatever the worth of that, certainly not dumbed-down philosophy. But definitely manageable by students and the like. It may be enlightening for professors and other teachers as well – some in science – and for all free-thinkers, philosophical and scientific, about the mind. Certainly it consorts perfectly with scientific method.

Anyway we now start again on our route, more slowly and carefully.

TWO

FOUR MAIN QUESTIONS ABOUT CONSCIOUSNESS

You're probably in a room. You're conscious in seeing it and maybe in hearing that electric hum and being aware of the support of the chair under you and where your left ankle is. You're also conscious in thinking the thoughts owed to these sentences. And no doubt you're conscious in having an attitude or two to things. Maybe a feeling about the conversational way this book starts, the pretending to be in a conversation with a reader, as the novelist Trollope does. Mainly with the aim, by the way, of getting a reader to keep in mind that the reader *is* conscious, has a real personal wherewithal for actually engaging in what is going on here, *is* in one way as expert as anybody else. Don't just sit back or murmur along.

So, as you've heard, there's consciousness in perceiving by the five senses, and there's consciousness that is just kinds of thinking, including *attending* to some bit of all you're conscious of in just perceiving, and there's consciousness that has to do with wanting in a generic sense – including feeling, desiring, inclination, valuing, intending, hoping, condescending and more.

So there's perceptual, cognitive and affective consciousness. That's an old division into three sides, parts or groups of things that make up consciousness. But it may last longer than some of the stuff you read about computers and consciousness. Don't read into the tripartite division more than is intended. It isn't any of many old and elaborated claims about *faculties* or *powers* of the mind or consciousness, for a start. It's just three sides, parts or sets of elements of consciousness.

There are three questions, then, about what these three parts or whatever of consciousness are, their different natures. That remains so, by the way, despite the second and third parts being related to one another in ways that they aren't to the first part.

And of course there's a fourth main question, no less important, of what the three parts have in common. What is consciousness in general? What is all the fact or thing or stuff or property or state or state of affairs or relation or whatever? To be more careful, what is consciousness in what a good dictionary calls the primary ordinary sense, the core sense, no doubt the one we naturally use?

If you've spent time in this philosophical neighbourhood before, you'll have heard of another question that is at least connected, traditionally called *the mind–body problem*. That fifth question comes down, unless you have very advanced and possibly batty ideas about computers, to the consciousness–brain question. What is the relation between them? If they're not one and the same thing, how are they related?

That it has seemed to be such a problem is surely because of our own fourth problem, that of what consciousness in general is. If all consciousness is obscure, or if you are tempted by or indeed drawn to a puzzling idea or feeling about consciousness, you'll have to be puzzled about the relation between it and the brain. Certainly we'll find ourselves dealing with the question. Is it the case, by the way, that you find you have to deal with the fifth relationship question in order really to answer the fourth question, of what consciousness *is*, its nature?

There are still more questions for us, not all of them rightly described as subordinate. An unexpressed assumption of at least most philosophy and science, still not thought about enough, has had to do with the location of consciousness. *Where* is the thing, stuff or whatever? Is it *within* the thing that is conscious? Around there somewhere? The neuroscientist Susan Greenfield once said between sessions at a neuroscience and philosophy conference that consciousness is in the brain but in no particular place in there. Something or other like that has been at least a common, usually tacit belief. To this assumption of internalism, a few seemingly universal but very particular *externalisms* have lately been added, additions to or qualifications of internalism. It's said, for example, that what a conscious event is, what distinguishes it or individuates it, is what it is about out there. How far does that take you with the question of what *it* is?

Can it really be that getting started on the consciousness problems in the right way issues pretty inevitably in more radical answers to what and where consciousness is? Maybe our ordinary impulse that seeing something is a lot different from just thinking or wanting helps lead us to a more radical answer. Come to think of it, isn't that pretty likely? All seeing has to do with *out there*, doesn't it? And there's also the fact that except when the subject has been the completely general one of the nature of *all* consciousness, there has always been separate attention in philosophy and science to consciousness in perception as against cognitive and affective consciousness. Maybe for more than one good reason.

Another question additional to our four has to do with the idea or ideas of *subjectivity*, or in any case the word. It does indeed have something to do with particular persons or personalness or what you might call individuality, doesn't it? Virtually everything written or indeed thought about consciousness makes some attempt to clarify or fill in or imply something about this impulse. What we can perhaps call its most primitive form is that idea of a *self* within each of us, an inner entity, a *subject* in a special sense, a thing different from but which somehow *has* the consciousness. Maybe you have given that up, along with a soul. But there definitely is some fact of *unity* involved in a consciousness, isn't there, continuing through time? What is that one thing?

In starting out on all these questions, all these places where it is possible to get hold of the wrong ends of sticks, not understand a situation correctly, make a wrong assumption, we do of course have the dictionary entry on consciousness. We have what Searle rightly calls a common-sense definition of what seems to be ordinary consciousness – presumably the definition *must* be of ordinary consciousness since it *is* in common sense. Consciousness in this definition is states of *awareness* that we are in except in dreamless sleep.

That has the virtue of including dreaming in consciousness, which surprisingly is not a virtue of all understandings, notably what I'd say is the eccentric denial by the storied Ludwig Wittgenstein of Cambridge. But how much more virtue or use does the common-sense definition have?

Not much. *Awareness* obviously needs clarifying and defining as much as *consciousness*. Can it be defined without in fact depending on or indeed being the idea of consciousness itself? Without facing the same problem? Certainly there seems to be uninformative *circularity* in identifying consciousness as awareness. Searle rightly remarks that what we have in this ordinary awareness definition of consciousness is *unanalytic*: it doesn't reduce it to elements, doesn't explain it in that fundamental way. It won't be of help to us, either, as a general account, if it just adds in a reference to the three sides or whatever without saying a distinguishing general word or two.

Do you take our main questions about the three parts or whatever of consciousness as unthrilling, but the question about the nature of all consciousness as better, maybe because somehow deeper, a little French? Maybe existentialist or even post-existentialist?

Well, we can agree that the word 'consciousness' by itself and the all-in subject are somehow a little challenging. The word makes us all pause. There is indeed a strangeness about the subject. What *is* the whole thing, state, fact or whatever?

But could it be that you can't get to general truth about all of consciousness without giving separate time to each of perceptual, cognitive and affective consciousness, maybe coming to a more fundamental difference between the first one of them and the other two than does your ordinary philosophy of mind? Also, do you have to give more time to the three sides than the amount given by those various physicalists who say superiorly that the mind is just the brain, that consciousness is just neurons, is just all those innumerable neural connections? Just physical, whatever they mean by that generality?

And do you have to give more time to the sides than you get from the opposing brave spirits, not many of them them spiritualists but including a neuroscientist-philosopher or two like Chalmers – stronger successor to the pair who wrote a book called *The Self and its Brain*. I'm talking about all those opposing *dualists* who say the mind just isn't the brain, that they aren't one thing but two, or, a little more carefully, that consciousness isn't physical, isn't the physical stuff that consciousness is somehow connected or correlated with. There are *two* different things here.

As for Searle, Wittgenstein, Chalmers and the pair Popper and Eccles, and all other cited authors to come, details of their publications are at the end here, in the lists of Readings, either General or Inclusive, or by chapter.

Even though there are confident answers in both philosophy and science to the general question of what it is for a person, animal or maybe computer to be conscious, and mutual citation circles, say of kinds of physicalists supporting one another in print, and probably a kind of majority support in at least science for the idea that consciousness is just part of the objective or scientific world, there is also more than pervasive and sharp disagreement about particular theories. And, more than that, there is at least pessimism, or rather there are at least different pessimisms, about our ever really understanding what it is to be conscious – getting to a particular theory or analysis, which is getting to something beyond, maybe a good way beyond, a definition or an initial clarification of the subject.

Is this general and fundamental problem the cause of the philosopher-scientist Jerry Fodor's familiar despair about what it is for something somehow to *represent* or to be *about* or *stand for* something else – his despairing line that 'if aboutness is real, it must be really something else'?

Chalmers, independent author of *The Conscious Mind: In Search of a Fundamental Theory*, makes a distinction between the rest of the science of mind and what he is known for naming *the hard problem*. It is, he says, that of the relation of consciousness to the brain, what has been called, as you've already heard, the mind–body problem. But, you may take it, this problem for him and other people arises from or is owed to the prior one of what consciousness *is*, the problem of getting a theory or analysis of consciousness.

Chomsky, who is so really right about so very much in both linguistics and in the rest of the world, says alarmingly that there really is no OK question of the relation between something physical and consciousness – because science does not give us an answer anymore to what anything being physical is, what objective physicality in general is. It hasn't been anything like simple particles for some time – several centuries, in fact.

Dennett, brave he of nothing less than the book bravely entitled *Consciousness Explained*, says consciousness is something people don't know how to think about. Nagel, known for a leading idea of consciousness to which we'll be coming pretty soon, said that what he had that leading idea of is in fact an intractable mystery to us. Others say it's the last great problem, presumably greater, for example, than whether space and time have limits and whether we can suppose either that they do or they don't (the philosopher Kant said we can't).

And McGinn indeed became well known for saying about the problem of consciousness that we humans have no more chance of solving it than chimps have of doing quantum mechanics. 'How is it possible for conscious states to depend on brain states? How can technicolour phenomenology arise from soggy grey matter?' This got him the name of being the founder of *mysterianism*, although not without dissent from such citics as the necessarily rational personification James Garvey of no less than the Royal Institute of Philosophy, who asked exactly what we were being supposed to be fated never to understand.

I have the feeling that some of these pessimists about consciousness, if not McGinn, have forgotten about or not heard of the hardness of other problems in philosophy. Say just the general problem of right and wrong – and such possible answers as my own, the Principle of Humanity. Or the problem of the justification of inductive inference – *how* it is that we know from experience that some future events will be like past ones, that rightly struck matches will light and so on. Karl Popper at the London School of Economics thought he had solved that. Or the nature of time – say the relation of the temporal properties of past, present and future to the temporal relations of earlier than, simultaneous with and after? Or the problem of truth – whether truth is correspondence to fact out there, or just coherence between propositions, maybe in here, or, to give you my unpublished preference, just at bottom something referred to in a statement being as the statement describes it to be?

And have some of the pessimists about consciousness as unique forgotten about, or never heard about, the problem of *things in general,* say chairs or coffee cups, traditionally talked of in terms of substances or bearers of properties, less traditionally talked of as just bundles of properties? Or the great logical paradoxes, such as the one about the Cretan who says that all Cretans are liars, which if true is false?

But, whether or not the pessimisms in general about consciousness are right, we still have to agree that there is an awful lot of disagreement about consciousness. So there's yet another question, indeed one that should come first, before the four main ones, and around here will come first. Is all that somewhat depressing and certainly contentious state of affairs about consciousness, whether or not you call it real disagreement, mainly or significantly owed to the fact that people are not talking about the same thing? Not answering the same question? Talking past one another instead? Because there isn't what we can call *an adequate initial clarification* of the subject matter?

Our four main questions about consciousness and its sides and the various subordinate questions, and this fifth one about disagreement, are also those of a very long book of mine that asks for a very dogged reader, a reader more dogged than me. It is a very long book of which this short one follows the same course but is not just a precis. If this one reaffirms the general line of inquiry and argument of its predecessor, it has in it different thoughts, crucial things clarified, forward movement in conceptions, including of philosophy, a few more conclusions, and also new reservations, rue and a mistake or two corrected. In this it is like many philosophical predecessors – above all the greater books of lovely Hume, *An Abstract of a Book Lately Published, Entitled, a Treatise of Human Nature* (1740) and his *Enquiry Concerning Human Understanding* (1748) as against his original *A Treatise of Human Nature* (1739).

We can ask the general question about all consciousness and the particular questions about the three sides of consciousness, and also the various subordinate questions such as the consciousness–brain one and the location-of-consciousness one, in a certain way. We can certainly ask the questions in the way of main-line philosophy, Hume's way, indeed ask them right in main-line philosophy. That, in my view, is certainly not deep or baffling or factless thinking, let alone vision or wisdom. It is indeed a concentration on the logic of ordinary intelligence, of course not sole ownership of it, but a greater concentration than that of science. This ordinary logic consists in (a) clarity, usually analysis, (b) consistency and validity, (c) completeness, (d) generalness. It is a greater concentration on this logic than science for the reason that science also has other things to do. Is it safe enough to say, then, that philosophy is *thinking about* facts as distinct from *getting them in the first place*? Maybe.

And a happy reflection about this present brief inquiry and development as against that long predecessor. Could it be that the first aim of clarity for most of us is best served by exactly brevity? Might it be, in our ordinary form of life, in this human world, where few or none of us including authors are masters or mistresses of inquiry and understanding, that brevity serves all of clarity, consistency and validity, completeness and generalness?

THREE

FIVE LEADING IDEAS
ABOUT CONSCIOUSNESS

B y one count there have been five leading ideas about
consciousness in recent philosophy and science.

Qualia

Is there an adequate initial clarification in the first one, which is to
the effect that consciousness is somehow a matter of your having
qualia? These things are said variously to be the ways things seem,
or features of mental states, or experiential properties of sensations, or feelings, perceptions, wants or emotions – or somehow
similar properties of thinking itself somehow conceived, maybe
even what we are inclined to call purely logical or factual thoughts.

Sometimes qualia are taken to be those personal and of course
internal properties in our seeing and hearing and so on that in past
centuries used to be called *ideas* in a special sense or *impressions*,
as with those giants already mentioned of what historians of philosophy call empiricism rather than the giants of rationalism, more
about perception rather than anything else – Locke, Berkeley and
Hume. Or qualia are or are like the items in twentieth-century
English and American philosophy called *sense data*, things

internal to us, maybe related to real colours and so on out there in the world.

Dennett says qualia are *the ways things seem to us*, the particular personal, subjective qualities of experience at the moment. Nagel says qualia are features of *mental* states – presumably he means conscious states. Very unlike Dennett, he says it seems impossible to analyse them in objective physical terms, make sense of them as objectively physical – whatever it is to be that.

Block for his part has it that qualia include not only *experiential* properties of sensations, feelings, perceptions, wants and emotions, but such experiential properties of *thoughts*, anyway our thoughts that are different from what is taken to be the functioning of unconscious computers – just computation or bare computation.

As you have also heard already, Searle says of qualia as he understands them, maybe acutely, that consciousness right down to the ground, *all* of consciousness, is just qualia. His point, presumably, is that the character or some character assigned to qualia is something had by all of consciousness.

Well, then, we don't get a first clarification of consciousness here with qualia – because of the disagreement about the damn things, including whether they're physical or not.

But, even more fatally, we also don't get a clarification since it's agreed from the start by almost all or most of the enthusiasts who have been called qualia freaks that there is *more* to consciousness than qualia. There's something else already touched on. That is what you can call pure thinking, sometimes called *propositional attitudes*, usually supposed to be without qualia. That very sentence, like any sentence here, expresses one. You can't begin to have a clarification of a subject that leaves out half of it.

That's not quite all. Qualia are given to us as *qualities of* consciousness, not what *has* the qualities, not consciousness itself.

That's what we want to know about, isn't it? Anyway, we want something like all the qualities.

Something it's Like to Be Something

What about Nagel's leading idea, for which he generously gives some credit to the English philosopher Timothy Sprigge? The idea laid out in the paper 'What is It Like to be a Bat?' is that something's being conscious, a bat or you or maybe some future computer, is the fact of there being *something it is like to be the thing in question*. Indeed, as Nagel also says, *something it is like* for *the thing to be the thing*. Sounds good, but for how long?

As indicated already in passing, about the definition of consciousness as awareness, you can't explain what it is to be a horse by saying it's something equine, or say what it is to be a dog by saying it's something canine. That's just circularity – an explanation of the term X that depends on what is or is effectively an equally unexplained occurrence of the term X or a mere equivalent.

What does it come to to say *being conscious* is just *there being something it's like to be the thing*? Compare being told that *being water* is *there being molecules and so on*. Or that *being a number* is *there being an arithmetical value*, where the latter fact is independently explained. What comparable instruction, what news, is given by saying what is said about being conscious? In the absence of anything else, you've got at least to worry that what we get here is just that being conscious is *there being something it's like to be conscious*.

What else could it mean? No new information there. Searle, although tolerant of the Nagel idea, in effect points to the fact when he says we are to understand the essential words in such a way that there is nothing it is like in Nagel's way to be a shingle on a roof – that is, understand them in such a way that that they don't apply to something we understand and take as not being conscious.

Also, about this second leading idea, you can worry in particular that no *reality* is assigned to consciousness here, by speaking of what it's like to be something. We know consciousness causes physical things. Could there conceivably be that causing without what Nagel declined to provide in his paper, some or other assurance of *physicality* with respect to the fact of something it's like to be something?

We'll be coming back to the large general question of consciousness and physicality – kinds of physicality.

Traditional Subjectivity

This third idea, an old one, is the idea we've passed by already that there are *selves*, that *you* in a sense are a *self* and that consciousness can be understood as what is of or had by a self. The idea isn't improved by being called the idea of a *subject* in a special sense, or a homunculus or small inner person, or an ego, or what *really* has your thoughts and feelings. Or something that has the very special freedom that is free will or origination or creation unaffected by causation in that it is no effect at all, or who *you* are in some special sense other than an ordinary one that at least includes a body.

Any self has to be distinguished from the rest of a thing that is conscious, the arms and legs and so on. How is it done? At bottom it's done by saying that it's *the conscious item*. Maybe, as already mentioned, what *has* consciousness. How else could it be done? But then we've got circularity again. That's not all. The philosopher Hume a couple of centuries ago, brave David, looked into himself and said he couldn't espy his self within the other stuff. Has anybody been successful since? Not me. You?

I'm not saying there is no sense in all the talk and impulse of subjectivity with respect to consciousness. It's all over the place in the books and papers. It's lurking there, isn't it, in the talk of what it's like to be something? 'I' means something to you other than or more than just your body, doesn't it? There has to be *some* sense in thinking of subjectivity. Chairs don't have it. We do. A decent theory or analysis of consciousness will have to try to find it – and give it the importance or size it seems to have.

Aboutness

The fourth idea is that prominent long-runner left over from medieval philosophers but kept more than alive by Tim Crane. It is that all consciousness is *representation* or *aboutness* in some sense or senses, also oddly called *intentionality* for historical reasons which we don't need to go into, and also *direction* or *directedness* onto objects or contents.

That consciousness is representation or aboutness, to stick to those names, can be and needs to be to say something not uselessly vague. It needs to say something rather specific like this: all consciousness is, anyway in part, fundamentally like the words you are reading right now. Or like pictures, maybe one on the wall of my room here, that good nude done by Ingrid in her drawing class. Those are things that *represent* or *are about* something else, *stand for* something else, *mean* something, in the way of all words and images and maps and diagrams and so on.

But, as has been rightly noted, consciousness includes aches and depressions having to do with nothing in particular. Whatever else can be said about these, maybe that the aches are somewhere in particular, they don't *stand for* something in the way of a word or drawing, do they? They can't only be about or of something in the funny sense, for example, that they are just *effects* of something, *evidence* of something. That would make rain conscious. Crane tries valiantly and inventively to save the aboutness view, but to me it is effort better spent in his own philosophizing.

There is also the problem of vagueness or ambiguity about those mentioned *objects* or *contents* in the story – despite salutary work by Christopher Peacocke elsewhere on the idea of contents. For a start, are mine to be understood as in here, in my head, or as out there? Or in both places? Might that third option be the best one? And whatever inner and outer objects are, how are they related? These are large questions.

One last thought. Does the aboutness tradition succeed in saying what its fundamental thing, *a conscious representation*, is? There's a pile of talk and problems here. And has the tradition spent time on representation in considering differences between perceptual, cognitive and affective consciousness? Maybe between perceptual consciousness and then cognitive and affective consciousness taken together? Would the tradition have stuck to the proposition that *all* consciousness is aboutness if it had?

Phenomenality

Yes, some consciousness is somehow identified by this property or character, according to the redoubtable Block in particular. Might he have said *seemingness* instead of phenomenality? He speaks of the concept of consciousness a little puzzlingly as being hybrid or mongrel, which could go some way to explaining disagreement about consciousness, and leaves it open whether he himself is speaking of consciousness partly in an ordinary sense.

But it is evident that phenomenal consciousness, although it has something to do with what he calls experiencing or sensing or directly apprehending, is close to or anyway related to ordinary consciousness. Other philosophers and scientists take phenomenal consciousness to *be* ordinary consciousness or imply it to be that.

There are quite few problems about all this. The main one is that phenomenality for Block himself is the property or rather properties of only one kind of consciousness, that *phenomenal* consciousness. For him, there's another kind. Block's other sort of consciousness is oddly called *access consciousness*. Chalmers calls this second sort *psychological consciousness*. What is it? Here is my pretty confident idea.

A split second ago, when you were reading a particular sentence about access consciousness, and, as we say, thinking about nothing else whatever, you *knew* – yes at that split second you *knew* – what your name on your passport is. And at that moment, when I was going on thinking about access consciousness, I knew the name on my passport is Edgar Dawn Ross Honderich.

Those things are true in the funny sense that there were then, as at other times, the facts about you and me that we could have answered the question of what our passport names were if we had been asked. We had what philosophers and psychologists have in the past called a dispositional belief rather than an occurring or an occurrent belief. There was a fact about us which most of us would call or agree to call *unconscious mentality*, an old and known subject to say the least.

I note just in passing what a book of philosophical and psychological essays has brought to my attention – that along with dispositional belief, there are psychologists who do indeed concern themselves with *unconscious attending*, although without using that very term. They do this without the benefit of an initial clarification of consciousness, and of course without a theory or analysis of it. While we can of course grant that there is research to be done into what can be called unconscious intending, or unconscious whatever else, let us persist in the ordinary use of talk of attention, where of course it *is* conscious.

To stick to our own subject now, you agree, don't you, that access or psychological consciousness is just the old dispositional belief or whatever, just unconscious mentality? Not consciousness at all.

So with Block and Chalmers, we have a first and striking instance of philosophers or scientists definitely not meaning the same thing as other philosophers or scientists in speaking of consciousness. Nagel certainly wasn't on about access consciousness in talking of what it's like to be a bat. How many more instances do we need in support of that idea that disagreement or whatever about consciousness is at least significantly owed to talking about different things?

But the main point now is just that phenomenal consciousness, or being conscious in the primary ordinary sense, say *experiencing*, is exactly unlike access consciousness. So we have one good reason for thinking we don't get a first clarification of all ordinary consciousness here. Also, is what phenomenal consciousness has, the property it has, as against access consciousness, a property not necessary to consciousness in general? Presumably so. Access consciousness doesn't have it. In which case, where are we?

Another question, unrelated but of importance. Does Block or anybody else *have* to concern himself or herself with ordinary consciousness? No, they don't have to.

Anybody can pick out what subject they want, use a word the way they want, anyway if they tell other people. You can take a word as a technical term. It's common. Descartes of 'I think, therefore I am' did that in saying what he also said, that other animals than us aren't conscious. He meant something true, about having language, which he wrote into his unusual definition of consciousness. So if we go on getting you to think about ordinary consciousness, consciousness in the – or anyway an – ordinary sense, not that we've done much thinking yet, does there have to be a reason?

We have a pretty good one already. It is that that is what you expected from the title on the cover of this book and a lot of other books and articles – unless you're a second-year psychology student also reading an old textbook. It's what anybody expects when somebody goes on about consciousness in any way and doesn't say otherwise. It's what we have to take or in any case do take any stuff about consciousness to be about if we're not told otherwise.

There's a rule of communication there. Maybe a rule of personal inquiry too. Anyway, we don't have to take and really can't take the subject to include your being conscious of what your passport name is when all that you were thinking about was a sentence of philosophy.

Still, as needs to be granted, psychologists or anyone else can choose and name their own subject matter, maybe best called *mind*, or *the mental*, no doubt for some pretty good reason. We need a reason for choosing ours – better than ordinariness. You can hope we'll get to such a reason, maybe at the very end. There and elsewhere, you can trust, we will be in accord with what the aim of main-line philosophy has always been, that concentration on the logic of ordinary intelligence worth mentioning again: clarity, consistency and validity, completeness, generalness.

Surely philosophy isn't something like *history* or peculiarly so dependent on it, as Bernard Williams feelingly supposed. And it isn't formal or mathematical logic either. David Hamlyn, a good and careful philosopher and historian of philosophy, wrote somewhere, surely rightly, that formal or mathematical logic has solved no philosophical problem, or maybe no large philosophical problem.

So much for a few words of summary of the five leading ideas. Now a few more propositions about them.

The first is that it sure is notable that Chalmers bundles all the five leading ideas together. He takes them all to come to much the same thing, to pick out approximately the same class of phenomena. He is not the only scientist of that habit. But evidently the ideas are different. Certainly the essential terms – *qualia* to *what it's like* to *subjectivity* to *aboutness* to *phenomenality* – aren't near to what he calls synonyms. And, certainly, if there's one class of phenomena there, it would be good to hear about it. What's that general class? That's our own main question of course, shared with a lot of other people.

Secondly, about the five leading ideas, is it not only the case that none of them provides an adequate initial clarification of consciousness, but that a comparison of them in their striking variety itself indicates again the absence and lack of a common subject really discerned? No shared clear question? I'd say so, despite that mention of one class.

But thirdly and more importantly, the five leading ideas were good ideas and worth the attention and respect that they have got – like the philosophy and science informed by them or motivated by them. There is no doubt of that. It brings to mind that in science there is the fact of respect for *consensus*, informed general or pretty general agreement, which is sometimes written into accounts of scientific method. It is written in despite its being otherwise describable as democracy about truth, which is not as arguable as some democracy or other in societies.

So, given the attention and respect for the five leading ideas, my spiritedness in dispatching them really has to have something added to it, right now.

FOUR

A DATABASE

We do not just discard all that philosophy and science of mind just glanced at – the five leading ideas. If you go through the published philosophy and science on qualia, what it's like, subjectivity, intentionality and phenomenality, you can get well on the way to what is the first of the main things in this present book.

This is a good moment, maybe the best, to remind you as a reader that your own attention to your own consciousness, your thinking along for and about yourself, is essential. This recommendation to engage in a piece of what used to be given the disdainful name of *folk psychology* is about as good for your purpose of truth as psychologist-psychology. Maybe you can use the reminder too that in reading a book by a philosopher you are not in touch with a higher being, but as likely a lower.

If you read those philosophers and scientists of the five ideas you find them coming together in a way. They use certain terms and locutions, certain concepts or conceptions – think certain related things without stopping to dwell on them. Suppose, as you very reasonably can, that those fellow workers or almost all of them are talking about consciousness in the primary ordinary sense. They think about it in a certain way in passing, use certain language for it, have certain concepts. For all of consciousness – perceptual, cognitive and affective consciousness.

Further, and of course very importantly, this is shared with other philosophers and scientists otherwise concerned with consciousness and with what they call the mind. You can be pretty confident that it is shared with you, that it goes with your attention to yourself, your hold on your own consciousness and your own logic.

What it is, to repeat, is that if you read the philosophers and scientists of the five ideas in question, you find them saying certain things, using certain ideas in passing. They do indeed share this with other philosophers and scientists, say one who wrote a seminal book on physicality and mentality in general, and a contemporary thinker on the subject, and a scientist whose subject is the theatre of the mind, and so on. They share it with philosophers and scientists who talk of consciousness being *experiencing* – where that is not only a synonym for *being conscious* but a gesturing at a process, a process with a certain character. And there are some of our fellow workers who talk of *being aware*, where that is not just the same thing as *aware* but some fact that is more than that.

The same is true, to remind you of it again, of those ordinary people whom some of my fellow workers did indeed used to call *naive subjects*, *folk* or *the folk*. Presumably, by the way, folk not excluding acute novelists and High Court judges and able schoolteachers with good degrees and sharp salesmen and other persons also pretty good at attending to, when they put their mind to it, what William James rather understated as their streams of consciousness.

So – the exponents of the five leading ideas and other professionals and the rest of humanity say things in passing or anyway

they will assent to things that are the result of their having holds
on their consciousnesses. A good selection of these things can be
put together from from books and articles. They are not thought
up or manufactured by me or anybody else. They're certainly not
from just my own hold on my consciousness.

Your being conscious right now in the ordinary sense, in any of
the three ways exemplified by seeing rooms, thinking of a name,
and a want that comes on you, is:

something's being *had*, the *having* of something,
something's being held, possessed, or owned,
the experiencing of something,
a stream had or experienced, not anything else, not anything
    underneath, not any such process, not any unhad condition
    of it
something experienced, only subsequently theorized about
    as qualia or whatever,
something of you, maybe *spoken of* as subjective,
something sensible, i.e. sensed,
something directly apprehended,
your seeing, thinking, wanting also in an ordinary sense
    of those transitive verbs,
something's being in contact, met with, encountered,
    undergone,
awareness of something in the sense of its *being there,*
something's being immediately in touch,
something's being apparent or obvious,
something's being close,
something not deduced, inferred, posited, constructed
    or otherwise got from something else,
what is not a hidden structure underneath,

what is not information or information processing not then
   had etc.,

something's somehow existing,

something being *for* something else,

something being *to* something else,

something being on view, in view, in a point of view, maybe
   subsequently labelled as subjective,

hence something's being open, provided, supplied,

something to which there is some privileged access or special
   knowledge on the part of one thing,

something with which there is acquaintance, maybe
   subsequently thought of as phenomenality,

what involves an object or content, sometimes subsequently
   much elaborated,

something being given,

hence something existing and known,

something being present,

something being presented,

something being shown, revealed or manifest,

something being transparent in the sense of being clear
   straight-off,

something's being open,

something being close,

an occurrent or event, not a disposition or cause of such events,

something itself real,

something vivid,

something being vividly naked,

something being right there,

an object or content coming to us straight-off,

something being an object or content, *theorized* in terms
   of aboutness,

in the case of perception the world as it is for someone,
in the case of perception, the openness of a world,
something proximal, not distal,
something in the light, maybe a spotlight, onstage,
something with a qualitative feel, as with all consciousness
   right down to the ground.

All that *is* data, and it's a sure bet it exists in languages other than English. You can get some reassurance from the Germans and a bit from the French. Probably Latvians. It *is* a database. The result of an empiricism.

To glance back at and compare it to the five leading ideas one by one, it's not a medieval technical term in much dispute and a couple of later pieces of English although with work done around them, or a philosopher's excellent aperçu but still an aperçu, or a familiar or traditional idea or kind of common talk, or an uncertain truth based on a few words and images, or an uncertainty about a consciousness that seems to slide into unconsciousness.

Of course there are a lot of things to be said about the data list. One is that it definitely isn't circular – for a start, there's too much to it. Another thing is that you could try to group items into various sub-categories – which is not our concern. You could think about the list in terms of perceptual, cognitive and affective consciousness, which is not our concern now. There are also a lot of questions to be asked about the list.

The main one is the question of whether it rings true to you. Is it the case that your being conscious right now in the ordinary sense in any of the three ways exemplified by being conscious in seeing a room, or thinking of a passport name, or a want that comes on you – is it the case that those things have the characteristics or such characteristics as those on the list?

The list isn't served up as a proof of anything. There aren't really proofs in philosophy, despite good tries like the one by the Australian philosopher Frank Jackson, subsequently withdrawn by him – about Mary the blind-from-birth neuroscientist who knows everything about the brain but then encounters something new by getting her sight back in the world of colour. Anyway there are no proofs in philosophy in answer to large questions, of which what it is to be conscious is certainly one – about which lack of proofs Jackson now agrees. That is one reason, by the way, why in my opinion philosophy is harder than science – and maybe makes less progress, as Chalmers says not too gloomily.

Asking whether the list of ideas or reports or impulses about consciousness rings true also isn't asking whether it is the explicit truth of the *nature* of anything, in particular the fact of consciousness really thought about, really made explicit. It isn't the kind of thing you have heard of earlier as a theory or analysis or developed account of the nature of consciousness. We are trying to get to one of those. That's the job in hand. It will take time, if not nearly as much time as in that labouring volume of which, as you have heard, this present book follows the same course but is more than a precis.

I really do not ask you a lot more about the database than whether it has the right ring. If you stand up and say no, you can be referred to further reflection on the exponents of the five leading ideas, when they are not on duty with their own particular ideas, and on those many other respected characters, more than can be noted, from primary schoolteachers upwards to judges making judgments about the awareness in the crime of the man in the dock. You can also be referred to just about anything said or written about ordinary consciousness in the main, ordinary sense when what is on offer is generality and not any product in theories or analyses. That is to say the prior and necessary indicators of what the subsequent theories are of.

Is the list just a laundry list? Just a long list of items that don't come together informatively or instructively? Well, it's early days to say it's not instructive. The main question of that kind is the question of whether it issues in or gives rise to a good or strong or arguable theory or analysis. But something can be replied now to the laundry-list question.

The list has in it things of what you can call two natures or characters: ontic or existential and also epistemic. That is, it is both about something existing and also about a relation having to do with a kind or maybe kinds of knowing or whatever of something existing, with the knowing or whatever including a knower or the like, a relation to something of that sort. In terms of traditional main parts of philosophy, the list brings together ontology and epistemology. This is true of virtally every datum despite the evident predominant character of particular ones as either ontic or epistemic.

Do you, being a tough cookie, maybe an American postgraduate hardened up in reaction to funny ideas at Harvard, say that you don't like mixed lists? Well, why is that? Have you discovered some principle to the effect that raw data can't be mixed? The principle isn't noticeable in the books on science and scientific method for the likes of me. If it turns up somewhere, we won't have to fall over. There's mixed data about evolution, football, women, lectures, lecturers, maybe everything.

The list, and of course the five leading ideas and a lot of other philosophy and science of mind, at bottom maybe all of it, bring to mind something else. That is *introspection*, which has been heard of a lot in the history of psychology. Maybe you say that's where the list comes from.

No doubt in German psychological laboratories of the nineteenth century the people who were the subjects of experiments were asked to do things they couldn't do, peer into themselves and maybe come up with stuff that would make for quantitative results in the psychology journals. The published results were not impressive. Those laboratories are no longer with us. Even Wikipedia on introspection is sufficiently informative about this, but look at the long and fine piece by Eric Schwitzgebel online in *The Stanford Encyclopedia of Philosophy*.

I ask you something related but unchallenging. Take the cases of (1) your being aware of the room you're in right now, or (2) your really thinking right now of a passport name, or (3) your being in a bad temper with someone who has just tried to be condescending about your country or your supposed social class or your moral politics. If you're asked what one of the events or states or whatever came to in general terms, what it shared with the other two events, what do you say? Do you say that *that* can't be got into general words at all? That what it comes to is nothing clear? That what comes to mind is hopelessly vague? Just a blur? Do you say you just don't know what to say? That *anything* you say is as likely to be wrong as right? That it's no better than a contradiction? That the things in the database just don't work at all, don't come together at all?

Of course you don't. It's not as if you simply can't compare the conscious events (1) to (3), remember sameness as well as difference. It's not as if all the terms and usages in the dictionary for our conscious lives, from being aware of to wondering to resenting to raging, whatever the circularity problems, have suddenly lost their meanings, can't be generalized about. And, to stick to the main point, it's not as if the things in the database don't work at all, don't come together. But this can be cut short with a couple more general propositions.

We can stick to the proposition already heard in passing that you do have a *hold* on your consciousness. What that means, for example, is that you can recall right now what it was a second or a few minutes ago to be aware of a room, or thinking something, or wanting something – and, crucially, that you can recall what they were like in general.

You can certainly test your recalling against the list of stuff in the database. There is experience available to you, whatever psychology and neuroscience do in going on to explain the fact. You certainly don't just go blank when you're asked to recall what it was or was like a second ago to . . . You can say things that have persuasive force.

There certainly isn't much chance of self-deception or mistake with the general question, with the recalling the nature of a moment or episode of consciousness. Maybe the only people who aren't to be trusted are philosophers and scientists who come to the question already burdened with an answer to the question of what consciousness is – or those people who can't stop theorizing in advance, maybe those who still remain Freudians.

Come to think of it, it would be slightly crazy to say that those five leading theorists of consciousness were originally on about what in general they-knew-not-what, a fact of which they had no decent experience. Where did those theorists get those leading ideas then? Certainly *they* couldn't and wouldn't have said they had no decent source. They might have wanted promotion to full professor or privatdozent or something, but they weren't, when they were on the job, just innocents or misled imaginers or self-deceivers or self-promoters or frauds. There must be a related proposition about the scientists of consciousness.

It's important that the list of stuff, to repeat, isn't just a good idea, like each of the five ideas. It isn't just something somebody came up with. It isn't elusive entities like qualia. It isn't an aperçu, an illuminating making of a point. That was the contribution having to do with there being something it's like to be a bat. The list isn't a traditional obscurity like the inner metaphysical self or subject, or a too narrow idea of consciousness prompted by thinking about words in language or photos, and it isn't the complications of the idea of phenomenality – not to mention the bundling together of all the five ideas in the way of Chalmers, who says very originally, you are reminded, that all that stuff consists in synonyms. Did he, by the way, just overstate something we may get to?

What we have in our list of stuff is indeed *data*. It is indeed a linguistic and hence conceptual *database*, maybe reasonably called a *databank*. Maybe you can deposit something yourself.

With this subject, consciousness, there is our holds, what we might call first-person empiricism. With this subject, unlike any other that comes to mind, each of us is in command of a fact of common humanity. Relying on it is consistent enough with the project of philosophy – that persistent use of the logic of ordinary intelligence. It is hard to see much vulnerability to self-deception or self-interest here, anything unusual in the line of not being subject to truth, anything chancy about my inviting you to trust yourself in the joint project of this inquiry. Unless Freud is brought into the room, which for good or bad he isn't. I say good myself.

Another thing that has to be said is something that may at first put you off. It may have put you off already. Yes, the list is metaphorical or figurative. Take a couple of obvious cases, starting with the first line. To say that with consciousness something is *had* isn't to say it's had in the sense that money or ankles are had. To say that something is *close*, not to mention McGinn's idea of something being *vividly naked*, is not to speak literally.

Well you are reminded here, scientist or whoever, that the history of science, as books of that history remind us all, is importantly or anyway significantly the history of progress beginning from metaphor. My suggestion to you is that here may be a further way in which philosophy can learn from science, indeed the method of science.

Don't forget either the role of metaphor in ordinary intelligent inquiry. A judge certainly finds out something about the defendant when he believes the witness who says the defendant always was a lion when annoyed. You didn't understand nothing, by the way, when you heard that we each have a *hold* on things in our conscious lives. But the really crucial fact with the database is that the proof of the pudding will be in the eating. Does the figurative database, no doubt with whatever other help we can lay hand on, issue in what is certainly different, a perfectly literal theory or analysis of ordinary consciousness? If it does, and if that theory stands up, it certainly won't depend entirely on the database. But what better start can we have?

Not important, anyway not essential, but can it turn out that you can argue *backwards*, so to speak, from the persuasiveness of a theory or analysis to the use or worth or importance of a database? Neither scientific method nor philosophical method is as simple as some might like them to be. It must be that the fact that something like a generalization really works in some independent way is a kind of confirmation of the data from which it came. It can put in question other data.

We need a summary or encapsulation or maybe a name of the database, just a way of referring to it. Let us say again that it adds up to an account of consciousness as *something's being actual*. That is no more circular, for a start, than your own name.

The database, we shall also say, is a preliminary clarification of ordinary consciousness as being *actual consciousness*. A first understanding of ordinary consciousness as *actual consciousness*. Consciousness that is understood as having those characteristics.

No, not a theory or analysis of ordinary consciousness, not the one we will indeed call *Actualism*. But a necessary start on the way to it. Yes, by the way, the words *something's being actual* might themselves have turned up within the database itself. There's a grammarian's term for that kind of thing. We are using those words, though, as you have just heard, as a summary.

One more question again. Is ordinary consciousness, consciousness in the primary ordinary or core sense, what we have now understood as actual consciousness, the right subject? If you want to think in this neighbourhood, think somehow about consciousness, is ordinary consciousness, actual consciousness, the right thing to think about? There are other possibilities, including Block's combination of what we can now call actual consciousness and also access consciousness.

We will have to consider whether our subject is the right one. But not now, not when we haven't yet got anywhere much.

FIVE

MIND-BRAIN DUALISM, ABSTRACT FUNCTIONALISM

You can get into trouble or anyway embarrassment if you collect your journal papers on consciousness into a book that doesn't pay much attention to fellow workers in the field. At least partly for that reason, you can get a magnificently bad review, say by that same Colin McGinn, bad enough to be written about afterwards by the *New York Times*. But there is a much better reason for always paying attention to your comrades.

You can not only learn things, but see what has to be done, see what has to be done better – whether or not you can do it. For any of us to succeed, to get to success with respect to a theory of what it is to be conscious, we need to see and assemble what criteria of adequacy a good theory will have to satisfy, the tests it has to pass.

Not that we haven't got a couple of those already. We are look-ing into ordinary consciousness, actual consciousness, which we understand to be the consciousness that is something's being actual – consciousness having those characteristics in the database.

OK, there are two questions. *What* is actual? And what is it for that *to be actual*? What does being actual in this sense come to in general terms rather than in terms of the initial list of characteris-tics? A good theory of ordinary consciousness will have to satisfy the criteria of answering those two questions. They're fundamental. They will be the largest questions in front of us, maybe with different answers for the three sides or whatever of consciousness, more different for the first as against the second and third taken together. But certainly those two criteria are not the only ones.

Consider the existing theory usually called mind–body dualism, which we were in the neighbourhood of back when we noted one of the five leading ideas of consciousness: traditional subjectivity. Dualism has a long history, starting before Descartes in the seventeenth century, despite his often being mentioned as its main historical exponent. Now sometimes taken as a benighted relic, dualism is said to be the proposition that *the mind is not the brain*. They are not one thing. They're two things, two different things. Dualism is the philosophical rendering of common-sense belief, right there in language, that there is mind and there is matter, a belief written into dictionaries when they define matter or physicality as what is distinct from mind or spirit.

Dualism, in a sentence that is only slightly more careful, is to the effect that consciousness is *not physical*. It isn't physical in the ordinary objective or scientific sense, or some objective or scientific sense, like chairs or brains. The proposition is embraced without expending much effort at understanding what physicality or physicalities come to and hence what consciousness is not. Whatever else may or may not be believed of consciousness in dualism, say that it is somehow a matter of representations or aboutnesses, this does not distract dualism from its main proposition of non-physicality.

There have been and there are leading philosophers and scientists who are in some sense dualists. Eccles and Popper, the first of whom got a Nobel Prize and the second of whom believed he had solved the problems of what science is and what induction is, what justifies us in thinking that some of the future will be like the past, wrote that book together called *The Self and Its Brain*.

Chalmers, neuroscientist as well as philosopher, and, as you'll remember, the author of *The Conscious Mind: In Search of a Fundamental Theory*, is a better class of dualist now, and/or if also one tempted to panpsychism, usually spoken of as *mind* being an inner feature of anything and everything, including lettuce leaves and teacups and drawing pins. Has Block been a fellow traveller with respect to dualism? There are other more metaphysically explicit dualists, including the quite sane Howard Robinson.

Dualism, to which we cannot think of doing justice, comes in two kinds, however important the fact is, one kind being what is called *substance dualism*. This first kind is pretty much to the effect that we have those *selves* – inner or metaphysical selves, sometimes called *subjects*, sometimes understood as having the special freedom that is free will or origination, noted earlier in connection with the traditional idea of subjectivity. These are non-physical substances or entities, things that have or are the foundations of the various properties of things. If you try to look into yourself, are you any more successful than Hume was in finding such a self? The second kind of dualism, *property dualism*, very different and a lot less developed, is to the effect that there are non-physical properties of things, always or usually taken as properties of physical brains.

There is, it seems to me, an overwhelming general proposition that can be stated quickly against dualism of either kind. It's that your consciousness, like mine, came into existence at some time, whatever problems there are about saying when, and it will come to an end at some time. That's called death. Also, it came into existence somewhere, certainly not nowhere or everywhere. So who around here has the nerve to say it was and is outside of space and time? Not having the nerve to say that is a good start towards taking it to be somehow real now, something that exists, a causal fact.

It's a funny thing that an awful lot of goodish thinkers, the ones inclined to dualism, are officially inclined to think that the greatest fact there is for each of them isn't in the world. The greatest fact of each of their lives, like the greatest fact in mine, is somehow their being conscious. That consciousness, that stream of it, according to all those thinkers, isn't physical at all. It's not a reality in what surely is the fundamental sense.

OK, that is loose talk on my part. There's no precision in that talk of a greatest fact. Here is something related that is not at all loose.

It is, you will agree, a clear truth that consciousness has physical effects, starting with lip movements and arm movements and including cars going around corners and ships sinking, and so on. People don't ever get put in jail only for what their arms do but for the conscious intention. The denial of this, that consciousness in seeing things, and consciousness that is believing and desiring things has no effects, used to be contemplated sometimes only in Australia, where the sun is very hot. No doubt that has changed.

Elsewhere there is the *axiom* of conscious causation, the denial of what is called *epiphenomenalism*. That latter thing, simpler than its name, is only the idea that consciousness just *goes along with* what is different from it – brain states or events that *do* cause actions and their effects really do the causing. Consciousness isn't causal, isn't in that fundamental way explanatory, with respect to where you are right now. Which, you may just agree, in good American English, is nuts. A decent theory of consciousness will allow and respect and in fact explain the fact that consciousness is causal – has physical effects.

Come to think of it, there is a very English epiphenomenalist. Nice man, able. Norman Bacrac. He comes to lectures and says, Please prove to me that epiphenomenalism is false. There is the temptation to reply that there are always *ur*-facts, facts with which thinking starts. And that there is one around here, which is that it was your feeling of confidence or whatever that made your lips move. Is there really better reason to look instead at something else just correlated with or goes along with your feeling? Something supposedly really explanatory in place of what isn't, say your rage?

All that is not to say there is nothing to be said for dualism. There is a very large thing to be said for it. It is that it makes consciousness *different* from everything else. That is what we all take it to be. As our dictionaries say, matter or the physical is what is such that mind or spirit is different from it. Here we have another criterion of a decent account of what consciousness is. A decent account really must make it *different* – somehow different in kind – whether or not the difference is also a matter of degree and judgement, even if there is no litmus test for difference.

To come on now from dualism to something else, it is especially prudent, whether or not required by a respect for consensus, required by a democracy about truth, to consider the current dominant theories of anything. If you take the philosophy and science of consciousness together, certainly the current philosophy and science of mind, including cognitive science, you must then consider *abstract functionalism* – which you've heard of before and will again. That is the basis or main basis of cognitive science and what can be called computerism generally about consciousness and mind.

Functionalism, in a fast sentence, is that being in a conscious state or event is just being in one that functions in a certain way – in the special sense of being only an effect of some things and a cause of others. That the conscious state is effect and cause is is surely true, but is it *only* that? And certainly its being functional in that sense takes us nowhere, because it doesn't distinguish consciousness from a lot of other things – everything that happens, all events, if determinism is true.

But there is more to this functionalism. It definitely makes consciousness into what its advocates themselves call *an abstract kind of thing*. Block is especially clear and definite about this. Consciousness is abstract although it is said to be *realized* in a brain or whatever.

This abstract functionalism is owed to a large inspiration and to a main premise. The large inspiration is that we do indeed identify and to an extent distinguish types of things and particular things in a certain way – by their relations, most obviously their causes and effects. We do this with machines like carburettors, and with our kidneys, and so on. The main premise, more important now, is the proposition that one and the same type of conscious state, such as exactly and precisely the same thought or hope or whatever, can go with different brain states, go with more than one type of neural or other physical state. This is the premise of what is called *multiple* or *variable realizability*. It is to the effect that we and chimps and snakes and conceivably computers can be in exactly and precisely the very same pain, the very same conscious thought or hope or whatever, but it goes with or is realized in quite different physical states. You can doubt that, for several reasons. But let the idea pass, anyway for now.

In fact abstract functionalism shares the failings of dualism. This reigning general science of the mind and the old metaphysics of mind, the dead metaphysics according to the reigning general science and a lot else, fall together. The first reason is that both dualism and abstract functionalism share the great failing of making consciousness *not a reality*. Both dualism and abstract functionalism really deny that my little worry of flying right now after that recent plane crash is any brain state or any other physical state or event. The old metaphysics of the mind and the reigning general science of the mind surely fall down together in this respect.

They also fall down together, more clearly and particularly, in making your consciousness not a cause, not causal in any clear sense, with respect to your arm movements and that email sent about alternative travel arrangements and so on. How can my consciousness taken as an abstract thing cause my being on the train to Edinburgh? Evidently, just like dualism, this makes my consciousness epiphenomenal, something that of course will be said to have something or other to do with brain states but in fact isn't any of them.

There is a related but different point. Whatever else we think about a cause and a causal circumstance – the latter being the cause plus other conditions – we think cause and causal circumstance in different ways fundamentally *explain* the effect, explain why it happens. But the so-called cause that is my nagging worry, the abstract thing itself, has no physical properties or any other explanatory properties. So the shortcoming that my abstract worry doesn't cause my being on the train has added to it or contains the shortcoming that it couldn't possibly *explain* my being there.

There is a place within other and very different theorizing for something you can call *physical functionalism*. It is better, partly because it puts aside multiple realizability, which has been too popular by half. Does much of science in fact tacitly contemplate *physical* functionalism, which is true to its name? That is, does it identify physical things partly by their *physical* causes and effects? Sure. So what about saying that conscious states and events are partly to be understood in the same way? If we were able to escape the hopelessness of objective or devout physicalism about consciousness, but have another class of physicalism, higher or anyway different, we could maybe make some use of physical functionalism.

But where we are right now is in the position that traditional dualism has the recommendation of making your consciousness different in kind from chairs and other physical stuff, as does abstract functionalism in its own way, but both of them, not only traditional dualism, deprive it of reality and in particular of its indubitable causal efficacy. For the dualist and abstract functionalist, not tripping in that walk in Queen's Wood before lunch is explained a little by my shoelaces being tied but not at all by my consciousness in seeing the fallen branches on the path.

Has abstract functionalism been owed to other motivations than the pair mentioned – other than the inspiration having to do with our generally distinguishing things partly by their causes and effects and then the premise of multiple realizability? Does it have to do with admirably wanting a theory of consciousness that somehow ties it to a physical reality lacked by dualism but gives it an arguable and realistic or more realistic counterpart of the difference than dualism gives to consciousness?

You can say that. The trouble is that it doesn't notice that it doesn't and can't succeed. You can't have the tied shoelaces in particular lawful connection with what doesn't have reality.

There is yet another problem with the functionalism we have been contemplating of course – and with physical functionalism, whatever role *physical* functionalism may have as a *supplementary* fact in an arguable theory of consciousness. What we can call the *content*, the present *content* of a conscious state or event, can't conceivably be only its causes and effects. It can't conceivably be only past and future stuff.

Necessarily think of yourself, as I do. There is my heart lifting at seeing the dawn, helped by dear Will Shakespeare's perfect line about the morn, in russet mantle clad, walking o'er the dew of yon high eastward hill – in my case the hill with Ally Pally on it, that people's palace of London. Or the content that is that little pang of apprehension that one of these sentences is forgetful or a blunder, which very definitely isn't just about causes and effects of it. *Obviously* it's not only a matter only of past and future. It's right now. It's more right now than anything else in the world is.

There's something a little deluded around here at the bottom of functionalism, as there was in its antecedent called behaviourism, in brief that our thinking of conscious states has to be replaced by thinking of behaviour, say limb movements. There's something deluded at the bottom of functionalism, and I'm sure it isn't you.

Is the plain reminder of the delusion of it a little service by the ordinary logic of philosophy to a piece of science in its lesser concentration on that logic? Not that the reminder has been much needed since the time of a famous refutation by Chomsky, an awakening of several whole professions and their fans.

Do we also need the reminder as well that science does more than a little service to philosophy by most of its greater concentration on seeing the possibility of, forming questions about, finding, developing, proving and elaborating the factual? *Of course*. Science cannot conceivably be a poorer relation.

And a philosopher's last word on that multiple realizability stuff. *Of course* the same *general* type or sort of state or event of consciousness, common to you and chimps and snakes, say what we can *loosely* call fear or fear of attack or maybe embarrassment, goes somehow with different particular neural or other physical states. But does not the general type or sort but *exactly the same* fear or fear of attack or embarrassment go with *different* neural or other states? Does any biologist believe that? Any biologist except a wonderfully innocent one lured into and seduced by the philosophy of mind?

Not a question for armchair biology, certainly, but what do you think yourself? Maybe we can be trusted.

SIX

OTHER PARTICULAR CONSCIOUSNESS THEORIES

Having looked at the two types of theory of consciousness that are dualism and abstract functionalism, and by implication at the general type that is physicalism, there is still reason enough for something else. That is a bird's-eye view, even with the bird flying high and fast, of a collection of other existing theories or analyses of consciousness, all or almost all of them more particular than dualism, functionalism and physicalism.

One of a pile of connected aims of the flight, the main one, is to fortify the proposition we already have: that there are certain criteria that a good theory of consciousness will have to satisfy – maybe to enlarge a little on those criteria.

A second aim is that of providing a setting or surround for the theory or analysis to come, Actualism – the theory or analysis of the nature of the ordinary consciousness that is identified by a database as something's being actual. You do indeed get a better idea of a Land Rover or a lion or an ambition by being ready and able to see differences between it and the rest of the automotive, animal or philosophical world.

To these can be added the aim of conveying something of the large disagreement about consciousness, disagreement issuing in the pessimisms about understanding its nature, disagreement indicating a cause in no clarified common subject. There is no winning theory of consciousness. As they often say at half-time of an English football league game, certainly Tottenham Hotspur versus Arsenal, there is everything to play for. The consciousness game is nothing like over.

More aims of the bird's-eye view, of course, connected with the first one, the main one, are to gesture at or towards, certainly not spell out, grounds of objection to the particular theories, and to indicate what is expressed or implied by many philosophers of mind, McGinn for a start: the need for something different – a new theory apart from its predecessors, therefore something with a chance of being defensible.

The bird's-eye view will also at least indicate that the philosophy and science of consciousness, as already indicated, does not have in it large proofs, but only comparative judgements, reasoned inclination. And finally the view will convey in passing, if by my silence, a considerable and common shortcoming of theories, shared with dualism and functionalism, maybe a crucial shortcoming. It is that of not spending time on what physicality is. Could that be as wonderful, maybe as hopeless, as thinking about the football league without, say, getting clear about what a team is?

Non-physical Events or States with Supervenience – and Anomalous Monism

One common kind of attitude to consciousness, already half or nearly in view, is that it is not brain activity or the like, not the processes of neural networks, but something that stands in some particular kind of connection with or relation to the brain or the like. This was more or less in view when we were looking at the second kind of dualism, property dualism.

Maybe the most common particular attitude here has to do with what is called the supervenience of consciousness on the other thing. Quite often what that supervenience comes to is left unexplained. It is sometimes said that it comes to the idea that there can be no change in consciousness without a change in brain, and also that a neural state can be replaced by another one without a change in consciousness – that there is a many–one relationship between brain states and conscious states, which is something you have heard of before. Multiple realizability.

The simplest objection, insofar as theories or analyses of the nature of consciousness are concerned, is that consideration of only this supervenience does not give an answer to the principal question in philosophy and at least implicitly in science. That is the question, of course, of what consciousness is, not just the question of some of its relations. In place of whatever else may be implied in talk of super-venient consciousness – perhaps something about representation – explicitness is necessary. Jaegwon Kim, who has spent a lot of time on supervenience, is aware of this in his admirable writings. Also, we must hear more of non-physicality, inevitably via hearing more of physicality. We need to know this for itself and in connection with the criterion of reality for an acceptable consciousness theory.

Donald Davidson's theory named anomalous monism also includes the impossibility of a change in consciousness without a change in brain and the possibility of a different neural state accompanied by the same consciousness. What is added is that these facts are not a matter of what you would ordinarily expect, lawful connection – they are not a matter of scientific law, say causal law. There are *no* psychophysical laws, no such connections, no such dependencies of states of affairs or whatever.

To this anomalousness is added that consciousness and brain, conscious and mental states, are in some sense identical, in some sense one thing – there is *monism* here. Some commentators say all this is also or boils down to property dualism. All of it, to me and to some others, also boils down to an epiphenomenalism, but that challenge and dispute can be left to your own inquiry – well aided by Stephen Law. Instead let us finish here with something else.

Anomalous monism is to me a mystery, partly because of what is rare, American philosophical rhetoric. Still, its being to me a mystery may be a failing on my part. What is not a failing is the conviction that anyone's philosophical acceptance of a theory of consciousness, like philosophical acceptance of a theory of anything else, cannot be acceptance of a mystery. That is inconsistent with philosophy understood as that concentration on ordinary logic, in particular its commitment to clarity.

Union Theory

As mentioned a while back, there was something called the union theory of consciousness and brain in one of my previous forms of life. This, preferred by me to anomalous monism, included lawful connection between consciousness and brain, but the theory's uniqueness was that it took a conscious and a correlated neural event, a *psychoneural pair*, to be in a clear sense a single effect.

It had advantages over both anomalous monism and theories of Hilary Putnam and Tyler Burge, to which we are coming. It did not have the blessing of a database and another large thing or two. It was thought up. It is mentioned here in passing mainly to declare that that form of life is past. What we are on the way to is something absolutely different from the union theory.

We take with us the lesson that a good theory of concious-ness will include an account of the relation of consciousness to anything that is explanatory of it.

Mentalism

Remember the leading idea of consciousness that is phenomenal-ity. It involves the further idea that consciousness consists in two things, these being phenomenal and access consciousness. As you have heard already, there has been a general concern with mind or the mental in the recent history of the philosophy and science of mind – including work that also speaks of itself as concerned with consciousness.

In the view of the many philosophers and scientists outside this camp, outside the camp of what we can call mentalism, the camp's subject is both conscious and unconscious mentality. The first is understood as something along the lines of the five ruling ideas – qualia, what it's like, traditional subjectivity, aboutness, phenomenality.

Why *is* there mentalism? Why is there this running together of the conscious and the unconscious? One piece of an answer is that there is a general preoccupation in science with causal and other lawful explanation: explaining *why* something happens rather than *what* it is, its nature, whatever connections there are between the questions. And that this preoccupation can lead to not dis-tinguishing large parts of the causal or other lawful explanation of something, running them together. But I'm not sure about all that, and leave the question to thinkers on science.

What we ourselves have so far is a subject matter named actual consciousness, consciousness in what is at least arguably the core ordinary sense. There is of course nothing against thinking about ordinary consciousness together with what is in the related sense unconscious mentality. It is common.

The different habit of *eliding* the two, running any tolerable idea of ordinary consciousness together with what it definitely is not, concealing or avoiding their difference, is from our point of view a pretty fundamental mistake. It may be the mistake, terrible with respect to the logic of ordinary intelligence, of drifting off a subject, confusing a subject with something else that it is not.

Also, to say it again just in passing, what we have with mentalism is a striking instance of a full-blown theory where philosophers or scientists speaking of consciousness are definitely not meaning the same thing as other philosophers or scientists. Nagel certainly wasn't on about access consciousness in talking of what it's like for a bat to be a bat. How many more instances do we need in support of that idea about what disagreement about consciousness is largely or significantly owed to?

We will not make staying on the subject a criterion with consciousness, by the way, but only because it is a requirement of *all* decent inquiry, certainly a part of the consistency that is a feature of ordinary logic and thus of the concentration on it that is philosophy.

Naturalism

If the term is often used loosely, and in effect takes naturalism to slide into physicalism and empiricism, it has a clear and less wide use. Theories of the kind then concern things and properties that are open to the scientific method. A more declarative sort of this less wide use asserts that there only exist such properties. Certainly naturalism excludes the supernatural in the ordinary, vague use of the term, including the supernatural in philosophy.

Shall we be agreeing at the end of this inquiry into consciousness that it is a natural fact? Could be. The resolute philosopher of science David Papineau would advise this, he being a straight denier of mystery about consciousness and the author of a good and individual book, and with the philosophy of science in his past. So would we have the blessing of the sagacious James Garvey already mentioned of what has long escaped being known by the acronym the RIP.

But one of us will add that the subject matter has been one that calls for both the factuality of science and that concentration on ordinary logic that is philosophy. We will have agreed that naturalisms as distinguished do in fact overlap – and overlap with other things, mentalism for a start. We will certainly not be agreeing that consciousness is adequately understood only as what is natural. Certainly it needs to be distinguished from other natural things or facts.

While we are here, but not really as an addition to the criterion in question, think of what may generally go with naturalism – theories outside and inside science that are fertile, pregnant or progressive as against degenerating or dead. A philosophical theory of consciousness with that recommendation, a workplace, would be good, wouldn't it?

Aspectual Theories

These include panpsychism, double aspect theories and the neutral monism of Bertrand Russell. Panpsychism has a long history, the adherence of such great philosophers as Spinoza and the recommendation of philosophers very much alive, these including Chalmers of the hard problem and Galen Strawson, strong son of a strong father.

The aspectual theories do not detain large numbers of the rest of us – the rest of us who nonetheless should not rest complacently in democracy about truth. Have these theories been made clear enough? No doubt you ought to try to find out. Should you remember the vulnerability of consensus? In more cases than I do?

Particular Physicalisms

The many different theories, like the devout physicalism in general we considered, have the recommendation of clearly preserving the reality of consciousness, in particular its own causal efficacy with respect to physical events. They are parodied, of course, by those adversaries and some near-sympathizers who, as mentioned earlier, describe them as reducing our consciousness to soggy grey matter, meat.

One physicalist, the redoubtable Searle, also known for his thinking on intentionality or aboutness and for the most striking argument against functionalism or cognitive science, comes to mind quickly. His original central proposition was that conscious states, whatever else may be true of them, are indeed physical states of the brain, biological, but *higher-order* states than others – each higher state is said to be realized in and also caused by lower-level neural or neurobiological elements in the brain. Like the higher-level states of liquidity of water as against the molecules, and so on.

There was my retort to the central idea that there are an awful lot of higher and lower neural or biological items in the brain such that the higher are not consciousness. Think of unconscious mentality in general. But maybe more reading, maybe more generosity, is needed on my part.

Dennett comes to mind as quickly. To attempt, bravely and dangerously, a partial summary, the idea is that our now taking me to be conscious is your taking a particular *explanatory stance* to me, at bottom like stances we take to muscles, plants, weather, thermostats and other artefacts. These are stances in which beliefs, desires and other intentional states are somehow ascribed to things to explain their behaviour. This general kind of stance, like several others, nonetheless really takes the things to have only physical properties.

What to say of it quickly? Well, that it has to contain an admission, anyway a problem. It does not do enough to preserve what we have as a kind of axiom, that consciousness is indeed different. Do you say there is the problem of making that criterion clearer, giving it more specific content? Well, that has to be left to you. You're not supposed to be just a free rider on this train.

So much for two champions of physicalism. Left out are an awful lot of other combatants and devotees. Also left out, with more reason, is the general and inexplicit physicalism of the general practice of neuroscience.

The great question about these physicalisms, as indicated when we were looking at physicalism in general, is indeed that of whether they really find the difference of consciousness from the rest of what exists, whether they do adequately preserve that difference. Even if they are notable theories of interest, propounded by individualists of vigour capable of defence of their individualities.

There is the *higher-order thought* theory, abbreviated to HOT, propounded by David Rosenthal and Peter Carruthers – higher-order but nothing to do with Searle. It is to the effect that among our mental states, all physical, some are conscious in the sense that we have not only them but an awareness or thought about or of them – a higher-order thought.

Eliminative Materialism

There is the audacity of the neuroscientific Churchlands, Paul and Patricia, originally seemingly to the effect that it will turn out in a future neuroscience that there simply aren't any beliefs or desires at all as we folk know them. Consciousness and/or the brain won't in fact be that way. The real categories will be otherwise. Maybe all that was just a misunderstanding of eliminative materialism, as has been said to me by Patricia in an email.

There is the world authority on Kierkegaard and perfectly acute Scot Alastair Hannay's insistence that conscious episodes of a human life can only be understood by way of *the first-person point of view*, in terms of that point of view's notions, both epistemological and normative. To try to understand these conscious episodes in terms of a single objective physical world debases and even eclipses the point of view and puts aside real questions for both philosophy and science.

There is also what lacks that clarity, the wonderful elusiveness of *quantum theory consciousness*, understanding consciouness by way of an interpretation or interpretations of the mathematics of the theory, which to me and others is certainly an outstanding case of the explanation of the obscure by the more obscure. Very able fellows are attracted nonetheless. Paavo Pylkkänen of Helsinki and Skövde for one. Also Stuart Hameroff of Arizona.

Seemingly Universal but Particular Externalisms

All of the theories noted above take states and events of consciousness to be internal to what is conscious. These internalisms have the support, whatever it is worth, of consensus, maybe including what is not to be binned along with folk psychology, which has been something near to our human consensus, near enough to all of our culture. Stephen Priest is one who speaks for it – and for a *radical* internalism.

To these theories have been added what can be taken to be, maybe rashly, seemingly universal but particular externalisms. They seem to take *all* of consciousness in its breadth, in all of what we have called its three sides, as being in some particular respect external. They are wide and flattening externalisms. They also all take perceptual consciousness to include not only something external but also, presumably, representations of it.

Hilary Putnam declared, in a good enough headline for his thinking, that meanings ain't in the head. The meaning of 'water' *depends* on what science says about the stuff.

Tyler Burge cogently explained by way of the idea of arthritis in the thigh, where it can't be, that mental states are *individuated* by or otherwise depend on external facts, notably those of language.

Andy Clark argued that some representation with respect to consciousness is a matter of both internal and certain external facts – minds *extend* to the maps and other means by which we engage with the world.

Again to be madly brief, Alva Noë theorizes that consciousness partly consists in *acting*.

You must be deprived by one of real consideration of and objection to these existing somehow externalist and seemingly universal theories of consciousness. To what extent or extents do they just add to or supplement rather than replace other theories of consciousness – go with other internalist answers to the question of what all consciousness or principal consciousness is? That would be one of my excuses for just flying by. Also, do they assume, in brief, that all of consciousness in its three sides is objectively or scientifically physical? Certainly that is not denied. Still these theories are fraternally recommended to you.

There is a radically different externalism unconnected with these – one to come in this conversation. It isn't Putnam, Burge, Clark or Noë. It is a discriminating or selective rather than a universal exernalism. It isn't about what science says about water, or just about individuation, or maps and so on, or acting in particular. In one large part, it is an externalism without representation at all. If this different externalism turns out to be OK, it will be more a refutation of these preceding externalist ideas than a development.

So – Kim and Davidson and the other internalist theories all the way to the seemingly universal but particular externalisms of Putnam, Burge, Clark and Noë. Despite my negativity, do contemplate and read any of that sequence of theories that catches your attention. All of them are *philosophy*, none of them to be located in a bookshop in any country along with pop philosophy, philosophy potted, a science aspiring to philosophy, science-speculation, couch-stuff from Vienna or Hampstead, mind and spirit, spiritualism, religion, the merely feelingful about the universe, or the occult.

Anyway, so much for my bird's-eye view. The main help of it among all those mentioned at the start of the flight is six of the eight criteria for a satisfactory theory. An adequate theory of consciousness, as well as being true to scientific fact and the logic of philosophy, must give answers to questions about consciousness having to do with

what is actual,
what being actual comes to,
reality,
difference,

subjectivity,
three sides,
naturalism,
relations.

A remark pertaining to the first two criteria. It is that none of the theories flown over, because they at least mainly depend on the five leading ideas of consciousness, proceed from an adequate initial clarification of the question. We have had such a clarification.

The third criterion, the reality criterion, brings back to mind what you heard earlier. While all of these theories, and general dualism and abstract functionalism before them, are crucially or at least centrally concerned somehow with *the physical*, physical reality, by which they always mean and usually say objective physicality, they do not slow down to think about it. They never get away from the subject, but they do not come close to really considering what it is, going over the ground. Is that good philosophical method? Shouldn't we get down there, walk around for a while? Be pedestrian in more senses than one? We will.

There are also other reasons or motivations, such as the imperative of naturalism itself, and the simple reason that consciousness itself must have *something* to do with physicality because it is intimately bound up with the brain. And, remember, there's the implication of much of the database itself.

The fourth criterion: difference. The theories deny, slide past or avoid the difference we commonly make with consciousness, between all of perceptual, cognitive and affective consciousness as against everything else. Consciousness in seeing, and thinking and wanting themselves, as against, say, the solidity of chairs.

The subjectivity criterion. None of the theories, if memory serves me, both abandons the idea of a metaphysical self *and* gives some arguable alternative conception of subjectivity. That's essential, isn't it? Your consciousness is bound up with your being you, isn't it?

The three-sides criterion. In not paying attention to them, as you have heard, the theories give uniform or level, flattening, flat or indeed Procrustean accounts of all of consciousness – whatever they may *add* to perceptual *consciousness* about eyes, ears and so on. Why do they run together what the rest of life, thinking life, separates? What they themselves separate when they are not on the job of dealing with all of consciousness?

The criteria of naturalism and such relations as that one called the mind–body problem. Look back at the theories yourself with respect to these.

SEVEN

THE CHARACTERISTICS OF THE CHAIR UNDER YOU

D o you muse that being physical is a pretty boring subject? Well, it may lead to what isn't boring; may eventually wake us up. Maybe slowing down now about the physical is the way of really getting somewhere. Didn't even Einstein plod in order to do some leaping?

Why not spend some real time getting really straight what being objectively physical is? Why not act with respect to the provocation quite a while ago in the admirable paper by Tim Crane and Hugh Mellor 'There is No Question of Physicalism'? It was so titled out of the conviction that no adequate conception of the physical was available, certainly none to be got by exclusive reliance on science.

There are different kinds of definitions of things. There are excellent ones suited to a purpose – and there are preoccupied, attitudinal, persuasive, prescriptive, purposive, cheating and such merely political ones as of hierarchic democracy and some mad stuff in it. The preoccupied ones are typically partly owed to their makers and users being taken up with a line of life, profession or method. The various different kinds of definitions include ordinary dictionary ones, scientific ones, stipulative ones and those special ones of which you have heard – adequate initial clarifications of something.

We need an understanding of physicality suited to this inquiry, an ordinary and general one. That is, a kind of definition that is true enough to science but also reasonably and necessarily informed by our common experience in our lives – and one that at least aspires to the logic of philosophy. The definition will be explicit rather than theoretical, not high-flying, definitely not a bird's-eye view. It will indeed be at a lower level than, say, the strong philosophy on the physical that exists, say by the sharp Barbara Montero of New York or Herbert Feigl of the Viennese past, and more preoccupied work in the philosophy of science.

The definition will have to do with sixteen pretty obvious characteristics or properties. The checklist divides into those that can be taken as having to do with physicality, the first nine, and those having to do with objectivity, the other seven.

Shall we start with the fact that an ordinary dictionary definition of the physical takes it to be exactly the non-mental? Presumably in the sense of being the non-conscious – since, to be quick, the definition presumably does not intend to exclude the unconscious mental, the brain, the grey stuff, from the physical.

The definition rightly reflects the conviction that consciousness is different, but, to stick to the present subject, there is an immediate objection from our point of view to it and to anything that comes to it. That objection is that the definition depends from the start on a good understanding of the fact of consciousness, which of course is not supplied and about which, as you know, there is vagueness and so on in place of adequate initial understanding. The dictionary definition also begs the question of whether consciousness *is* physical, by denying it.

But is there something of value in this assertion of the physical as the non-conscious? We can better answer that question by delaying until we have looked at other characteristics first.

Physical Characteristics

Perhaps the most common definitions of the physical world in the philosophy and science of mind now, and certainly in the philosophy of science and in full entries in a general dictionary or two, relate the physical to science, often to physics. Shall we say that physical properties, whatever else they are, are properties asserted or assumed to exist in science? Or in hard or harder science? That faces several problems. What science? And, since we are indeed after a general and of course all-inclusive definition, we have to think something about the obvious question of what new and now unknown properties will turn up in future science. Here is a response, a first characterization of the objective physical world, a characteristic of it as physical rather than objective.

(1) Physical properties are those specifically or by implication accepted in contemporary science, counting physics to the fore – and those properties in future science of the same general type, such properties as can be anticipated on the basis of paradigms in or related to contemporary science. This first identification of objective physical properties and their natures, then, is that they are those in the inventory or taxonomy of present and related science. But, to my mind, there must also be a second idea connected with science.

(2) Particular objective physical things and kinds or categories of them are those whose existence and particular further natures are confirmed by the scientific method. Leave aside the interesting and somewhat controversial matter of the understanding of

the scientific method. Come on to the fact that indeed there has been a tendency, in particular within science and the philosophy of science, to suppose that the physical is definable *only* in terms of science and particularly physics – presumably in terms of both inventory and method. There have also been persuasively strong arguments against that imperial tendency. Not only because of the evident inexplicitness of the science-based definitions: there is indeed good reason to go a lot further. It is easy to suppose, for a start, despite the fact that the use of examples raises general questions, that you are perfectly confident that Mount Everest and the chair under you are physical, on account of their properties. Our coming reflections can be guided by such facts and reflection on them as well as by science. So there is more to say, the first thing very simple.

(3) Physical properties of things are properties that occupy spaces and times. This is the idea that a physical thing, a thing with physical properties, is something extended in space and time, which is to say for a start that it has size and shape and also duration. These properties, like others below, are such that first or further knowledge of them is by way of the scientific method.

Are both space and time matters of difficulty, problems themselves? Is time a problem with respect to the connection of the temporal properties (past, present and future) with the temporal relations (before, simultaneous with and after)? Are space and time also a problem for physicists who haven't heard of Immanuel Kant's contradiction or paradox mentioned earlier – that we think of each of space and time as both limited and unlimited? Yes, but leave all that to those who deal with the universe or universes, sometimes on television, and come on towards something more manageable. But note on the way, and remember with other characteristics to come, in connection with Chomsky's proposition that there is no adequate conception of physicality, that there are characteristics of physicality that certainly do not depend for their adequate specification on science, whatever it may add with respect to them.

(4) Particular physical events or states or things, anyway ordinary and indubitable ones, stand in causal or other lawful relations, dependency relations, with other such events, states or things. It is not too much to say that a hill absolutely without effects, beginning with the effect of its being seen, would not be a hill. Nor would a match be a match, or a neuron a neuron. The idea of a lawful thing is usually in part the idea of something that stands in a web of connections or relations with other things.

What, in general, are causal and other lawful connections? They are spoken of as dependencies, necessities, connections of natural law. They are, to be more explicit, connections stated by certain conditional or if–then statements. According to an elderly argument and view definitely not retired by me, they are to be understood in terms of what is basic to the rest of them, a foundation of all such connections. That is what is stated by certain special conditional statements.

These are not logical or terminological connections, evidently, such as *If he's a bachelor, he's unmarried* or *If p then q, and also if p, then q*, but very different conditional connections. They are connections reporting the way the world is.

The foundational ones, I came to believe a while ago in coming to a theory of determinism and a theory of freedom, are those stated by conditional statements of a certain general form. *If or since a first thing happened, then, whatever else had also been happening, a second thing would still have happened.* The second thing *depends* on or is necessitated by the first in that specified sense. There is also a dependency, which we need not go into, of the first on the second. If the second had not happened, then, ordinarily anyway, the first would not have.

The most common of such whatever-else connections between things are between causal circumstances and effects, sometimes called sufficient conditions and effects, where the circumstances or sets of conditions precede the effects in time. A circumstance may include a particular condition we may call the cause of the effect. Other lawful connections, connections between lawful correlates, are typically between things simultaneous in time.

The cause in a causal circumstance, of course, is distinguished from the other conditions not because it is fundamentally different – it is a necessary condition like the rest of the conditions for the effect – but on account of its being an attended-to part of the circumstance. It may be attended to for its unusualness, or for its manageability or other practical reason, or because it is not understood, or not as well understood as other conditions.

(5) To characteristic (4), which concerns the lawfulness of particular events or the like, we can add something you may take to be implicit in it, not about particular events or whatever but about categories of them. Science is pervasively concerned with whole categories of lawful things and sequences of them, however the categories or sets can be subdivided or added to. Indeed science is mainly concerned with such categories whenever it is not pure mathematics, mathematics unapplied to such things. So –

Whole categories of physical things, anyway ordinary and indubitable ones, stand in causal or other lawful connections with other such categories. Conditions for temperature or growth stand with temperature or growth itself, maybe conditions for understanding stand with understanding itself.

Do you know something or maybe a lot about physics and so press on me a proposition, or anyway a question, about particular dependencies as in (4) and categorial ones as in (5)? In quantum theory, are there not supposed to be chance or random things? Something like that is regularly said, or used to be. Is that to be taken as meaning that there are events or the like that are not lawful?

One quick reply is that the lawful connection of categories may be a mark of the physical even if lawfulness is somehow different in interpretation of the mathematics of quantum theory. Keep in mind too that lawfulness does indeed hold only between properties, events, states and the like, either particular ones or categories of them – in general *things that happen*. Certainly not between numbers or features of a calculation or whatever else.

Another quick reply to the quantum theory question with respect to (4) and (5) is that the interpretations of the theory, its applications to the world, are a mystery, as even sympathetic reporters say or even celebrate. There's no excuse in saying, as sometimes happens, whether or not truly, that the interpretations are *philosophical*. The competing kinds of interpretations of the mathematics, the attempted inconsistent applications of it to reality, are what a brave enough philosopher can call a mess. That is absolutely consistent, you will understand, with a general respect for science, a general deference, and indeed an envy and of course an insecurity.

To press on very quickly rather than defend myself, here are three more proposals as to characteristics of the objective physical world, all having to do with perception.

(6) Physical things of the ordinary or macroscopic kind, such as the ones in your room, are perceived in such ordinary ways as sight and touch – and certainly measurement. Other objectively physical things, down in what we can call the microcosm, particles and spin and so on, are not ordinarily perceived, but they

stand in lawful connection with what *can* somehow be ordinarily perceived, for example, with experimental results.

In passing – this connection with perception is only one reason for staying a long way away from the idea that the objective physical world is what Kant called the noumenal as against the phenomenal world, the world of things in themselves as against things as we perceive them, and depended on for a great deal of argument and conclusion hereabouts.

(7) Ordinary physical properties are perceived not from only one point of view or perspective. They are open to more than one point of view or perspective.

(8) Ordinary physical things somehow are different from different perceptual points of view. They have different perceived properties – sizes, parts, sides, aspects, relative locations and so on.

Now we can hardly just sail past the persistent subject of primary and secondary properties. The primary properties of things, for the philosopher Locke in the seventeenth century, were shape, size, motion or rest, solidity and number – into which we do not need to inquire further. Primary properties for those concerned with them today include more, not only Newton's mass but our small particles, spin, charm and so on – which also have to be left for your private investigation. The secondary properties for Locke were or included colour, sound, warmth and cold, and taste.

A fact about the two categories is that our perceptual consciousness of secondary properties is dependent on lighting conditions, point of view, distance, eyesight and states of our other perceptual equipment. The second and resulting fact is that of differences with our perceptual consciousness of secondary properties of a thing – say your seeing the colour of the bus differently from me as a result of your sunglasses.

These differences, incidentally, proved to the satisfaction of Locke the large proposition, no one-day wonder, or even a one-century wonder, that we do not get or have in our conscious experience one relatively unchanging thing, say a bus. We have in our consciousness only what Locke called *ideas* of it – images or representations of a related kind, maybe qualia, certainly things said to be in the mind, somehow subjective. You will certainly be hearing more about that, but what is to be said now is familiar.

(9) In short, ordinary objective physical things have the physical properties that are primary and secondary properties.

So much for physical properties of the objective physical world. Now note this world's characteristics of objectivity rather than physicality.

Objective Characteristics

First, something that brings back to mind that opening mention of ordinary dictionary definitions of the physical. There is the objective characteristic of the physical that it of course does not in certain ways involve consciousness if consciousness is taken to lack the characteristics above that we have already assigned to the objectively physical world. The objectively physical does not involve consciousness that is other than being in science in the two ways or occupying spaces and times or being in lawful connections, and so on.

We can look forward again to contemplating at the end a larger retrospective proposition – (16) – mentioning all the other characteristics of the objective physical world but the one we are now on about. Anyway, as for here –

(10) Objective physical facts are separate from facts of consciousness taken as non-physical – objective physical facts are not

themselves such facts of consciousness, do not include such facts and are not lawfully dependent on such facts.

Other characteristics of objectivity can be noted quickly.

(11) Objective physical properties are also objective in that, despite difficulties in practice, they can be a matter of the consciousnesses of more than one particular individual and hence are in this sense dependent on no particular individual. They are instead public.

Another proposition is one we also encountered in connection with one of the five leading ideas of subjectivity. It has to do with each of us having a certain greater confidence about our own consciousness than that of others, given certain usually reasonable assumptions. This at least stands together with a fact we began with, that we have a *hold* with respect to being conscious. So –

(12) Physical properties are objective in not being a matter of someone's or something's privileged access. This is persuasive enough without attention to what privileged access, where it exists, can come to. See for a real start the thoughts of Ernie Sosa on this troublesome subject.

To come on now to something different, there is the idea of objectivity that is to the fore in ordinary life. Certainly it cannot be left out of the philosophically and scientifically dominant conception of objective physicality we are assembling and considering.

(13) Objective physical properties are those whose existence and nature are at least taken to be what in truth and logic they are, not supposed properties significantly owed to prejudice or one-sidedness, not owed to any feeling or desire irrelevant to the facts, not owed to feeling or desire having to do with personal relations, gain, loyalty, or ethics, politics, aesthetics or other evaluative practices.

The next item takes us back to scientific method – considered now not in connection with physicality but with our present concern of objectivity.

(14) The physical as we are considering it is objective in that it is pre-eminently confirmed by the scientific method that includes clarification or characterization, theory or hypothesis, prediction and testing.

Now something quick about some traditional philosophy, in fact one of those five leading ideas, the third one, about subjectivity.

(15) The objective physical world does not include any self or homunculus or other kind of unity inconsistent with the characteristics of the objectively physical that we have.

It comes to my mind to add that we have as much reason, probably more, to exclude something else. This particular idea of unity has to do with a desire or conviction as to our human standing above nature or the rest of nature, an idea of free will or origination, that mysterious kind of freedom you heard of earlier, so different from ordinary voluntariness and connected with desert or retribution. All that is inconsistent, for a start, with lawfulness.

In my huffy judgement, origination and uncaused creativity and all that stuff needs to be regarded as part of the funny past. But excuse me here and now, as against a very late moment of this inquiry, any return to that preoccupation of mine in the past – determinism and freedom. Determinism, by the way, is indeed better called *explanationism*, or maybe *causalism*, which names convey that every event has a causal explanation but does not imply something darker than that.

Finally, come back now to something with which we started and delayed dealing with, the question of whether the domain of the physical we are considering is such that we must hesitate about including ordinary consciousness, actual consciousness, in it. A brief answer is possible, one that takes into account certain characteristics of the domain of the physical.

It is not easy to see that conscious events and states contemplated for physicality can persuasively be taken as (6) like particles and forces of the scientific microcosm in their reassuring connection with perception. That counts against a conclusion of physicality? In connection with (7), (8) and (9), all pertaining to perception, it is clear that cognitive and affective consciousness, thinkings and wantings and the like, do not involve a point of view, are not different from different points of view in the relevant senses, and do not have primary and secondary qualities.

Nor are conscious events and states public in the given sense (11) or not a matter of privileged access (12). And, as just concluded (15), *if* actual consciousness is taken to involve a metaphysical self, then actual consciousness cannot count as objectively physical. More tentative remarks might be made about other characteristics. But we can draw a conclusion now.

(16) Characteristics of objective physicality as listed above do certainly make for at least significant hesitation about taking consciousness in the primary ordinary sense to be objectively physical. There is this hesitation among the rest of us if we put aside those personnel who are hardened cases – maybe including those occasional scientists who have imagined that philosophy is not in the real world. But, on the other hand, if you go through our list, you find stuff that goes with and supports the idea – some idea or other – of consciousness as physical. *Of course* consciousness is within science, of course it has physical effects, of course it is rightly taken as lawful, by clear-headed exponents of its supervenience on the brain, among others.

There is time for two pieces of business, of which the first is that that it is a commonplace in philosophy and adjacent interested territories that objective physicality is the only physicality. The objectively physical world is the only physical world. There would be no problem about providing evidence of this commonplace. Nagel on what it is like to be a bat said 'whatever else may be said of the physical, it has to be objective.' That refrain has continued.

My response to that can and must be simple. Read on. Either another physicality will be produced and somehow justified or it won't.

The other piece of business. You will well remember that Chomsky in his pessimism denies the possibility of a conception or the like of the physical of a certain kind. Since the time of the physics of Newton, on account of what has since come out of it, up to contemporary physics, there is has been no such possibility.

My own uncertain understanding of what we are being taken to lack, the kind of thing, is that it has two characteristics. It is only from that science, and it is in a necessary way general. The state of our science is such that we cannot have such an instructive generalization.

You will guess my reaction to this, given our own thinking about the physical. That a general or summative account has to be restricted to nothing but science is not and should not be the case. Consult, if you feel urgent, Crane and Mellor, and Lycan, and Stoljar – all in the Bibliography. And, if you lift the restriction to science, while certainly making use of science in an account, you *can* have the needed generality. You get it, for a start, by way of ideas of space and time and of lawfulness and perception, not to mention the different consideration of the division of labour between science and philosophy.

If we are asking what consciousness is, and contemplating that it is physical, is there an argument for asking whether it is physical in the or an ordinary non-science sense? Well, that is certainly the ordinary form of the question. Is there an argument to the effect that this ordinary conception of the physical is somehow necessary to the existence of others? That is left to your private study. Of course a final proof of the pudding that is our account of objective physicality will be in the eating – in its contribution to an answer to the question of the nature of ordinary consciousness.

To bravely add a speculation in passing, there is *some* truth in the proposition that you learn more of what a problem is by contemplating its solution or proposed solution. Some uncertainty or mystery about a question may evaporate. Will Chomsky agree with that? And, more important, agree with a consciousness question, agree about it that it has sufficient clarity, sense, content, coherence? And agree with a consciousness answer? Let's hope. Helps as much with philosophy as science, doesn't it?

EIGHT

CONSCIOUSNESS IN SEEING: WHAT IS ACTUAL?

O n we go now – from that figurative database and the encapsulation of ordinary consciousness as something's being actual, and the pile of theories of consciousness, and the criteria for a better theory – starting with answers to the two questions of what is actual and what being actual is, and then our getting a plain understanding of objective physicality.

It seems to me and others that we need to make a real escape from the orthodox and indeed the less orthodox in the science and philosophy of consciousness. We need to break out, maybe make a leap. There is a fair bit of agreement about this. McGinn declares we need to kick our theorizing into a higher gear. Harold Brown speaks of the need for a conceptual revolution, as in physics. Others including James Garvey and Stephen Law say similar things in that volume of papers collected by Anthony Freeman for the *Journal of Consciousness Studies* on my earlier struggle or progress towards the present theory of Actualism.

Sitting in a familiar room in Hampstead once, I said to myself: Stop reading all this madly conflicting stuff about consciousness, past and present, say from the logical positivist Freddie Ayer to comparably resolute psychologists to mighty metaphysicians.

You're conscious. *You're* conscious right now. This isn't quantum theory, or Hegel, let alone the difficulty of moral and political truth, say in the honest work of Alasdair MacIntyre beginning from a German railwayman or in struggling work by way of some best definition of terrorism as conceivably including some good terrorism.

Just face and keep on facing the consciousness question. What is your being conscious right now in seeing this room? Not your thinking about anything or attending to something seen of course. Not your liking it or whatever. More particularly, *what* is it that is *actual* with your perceiving? You know the answer in some sense, don't you? You've got the hold. You don't have to be Einstein.

The answer in my case, lucky or unlucky, was that what was actual with my being perceptually conscious was the room's being there. In due course, some months later, being a slow thinker, I got around to thinking it might be better to say my being perceptually conscious was *a* room's being there, but that certainly didn't subtract it from being out there.

And in general what is actual with all perceptual consciousness is *a subjective physical world*. Being perceptually conscious is a subjective physical world's being there. That is maybe the main or most notable one of the various different propositions of the theory of Actualism.

More particularly, what is actual with all perceptual consciousness is a stage or space-time part of a subjective physical world. Saying so is a counterpart to familiar talk of being in touch with the world as ordinarily thought of, or the objective physical world, in virtue of being in touch in another sense with just a passing bit of it.

There is reason for the usage *a subjective physical world*, perfectly literal sense to be given to it. A lot of sense. Of course we need to come to know what one comes to, what its general nature is, what the true or best theory or analysis of it is. Certainly we need to get beyond metaphor. But we know a few things already.

For a start, there is one subjective physical world per perceiver. So yes, there are a myriad number of these changing worlds, as many as there are perceivers. If that leads you to wonder if they are a kind that really exists, or are a suspicious kind of thing, you can open an encyclopaedia of science. There you will learn of whole piles of things such that there are a myriad number of each of them. Start with particles.

Yes, the stages or space-time parts of any subjective physical world are also transitory. And there is change within a stage. So it's not easy to come up with a general principle for counting them, for saying where one stage ends and another begins. Like an awful lot else in science. Try that encyclopaedia again. Neither being one of a myriad or being transient makes something unreal in any relevant sense.

You may be ready to contemplate, now, whether or not with confident complicity, that *what* is actual right now with respect to your perceptual consciousness is a room or other place. It's something out there in space, as much as anything at all is out there in space. Yours started with your first perception and will end with your last one.

God knows my room is not a room *in my head*, whatever that would be, whatever that loose talk comes to. Anyway I know my room isn't any such thing. So do you know about yours. You walk around in your room, as I do in mine. The same goes for your whole subjective physical world.

With your being perceptually conscious right now, say visually conscious, is there *more* than a subjective physical world that is actual? Is there something else that is *had*, is *given*, is *right there*, is *presented* and so on? Does what is actual include more than a room or some other place? Well, certainly there are a lot of philosophical and psychological theorists who theorize that *ordinary* perceptual consciousness, however they think of it, however they get to it, definitely is a matter of other stuff. Ordinary perceptual consciousness somehow contains other stuff.

So – in your case, to ask our own first question, does what is actual with your perceptual consciousness now also include those *ideas* as they used to be called, the visual ideas of the distant philosophical past – Locke, Berkeley and Hume? Does it include the more recent *sense data* of Bertrand Russell and Ayer and sympathetic American philosophers?

Any recent variations such as the project of my London neighbour Paul Coates to go beyond the estimable American Wilfrid Sellars? Stuff from which you infer or deduce or reason your way to the existence of a room? Premises for that conclusion? Data in the sense in which our database was and is data but no more than data for our present inference to the very nature of consciousness?

Does it include any such internal stuff whatever surveyed in such excellent surveys of the history of the philosophy of perception as Howard Robinson's? Does what is actual with you now include the *qualia* you have heard of? Does what is actual with you now in seeing things include what Block defends or defended as *mental paint*? Does it have in it what is implied or contemplated by the original and Humean Jerry Valberg in what he calls the puzzle of experience?

Does it include *any* such internal stuff – any stuff not out there in space? Does it include anything that justifies more or less literal talk of a theatre of the mind with a spotlight, however useful and indeed inspirational to the scientist Bernard Baars? Does it include something called inner space, but *literally* a place, like a London square, maybe Gordon Square, as Richard Wollheim started out his professorial career by saying in his inaugural lecture?

Does it include what you can follow quite a few contemporary philosophers in calling a *content* or an *object,* maybe a *non-conceptual content*? – by which they mean or seem to mean an internal content or object, a thing in a mind, indeed *of* consciousness.

It has to be put to you that with your consciousness in seeing the room what you have, what you are given, what you are directly aware of, what is not deduced or got from something else, what is real and right there and so on, isn't any of this stuff. The only paint is the paint on the walls.

Whatever we come to say about your thinking about it on some occasion, maybe right now, or your attending to or picking out the computer in wondering if it is acting up again, or whatever we come to say about your wanting something with respect to the ruddy thing, that internal stuff isn't anything you have or are given now with your perceptual consciousness. Almost all or a great deal of that stuff flogged to us in connection with perceptual consciousness somehow ordinarily conceived is in fact, in a word you know, *representations*, sometimes *iconic representations*. Perceptual consciousness is what is about or of something else, stands for something else, points to it, is directed to or is towards something, is something that carries the mind to something, gets something other than itself into the story.

All that talk can be left loose and vague, which of course is no help. It has to be definite and clear, which it can be. It has to be to the effect, for a start, that the fact of your being conscious in perceiving a room consists of or has in it something like a word or sentence or picture or a map.

To put it to you intemperately, that plainly isn't true. We bloody know what it's like to have a representation in or with respect to my consciousness. It's like the experience of seeing that line drawing by my wife Ingrid up there on the wall: that thing that is *of* something in the familiar sense. The room that is given right now in my seeing isn't *of* anything at all. It's not a *sign* of something. It's nothing like your reading these words. We know when someone or something is sending us a message, even sneakily.

And what is *wanted* by me in various ways with respect to the room isn't wanting with respect to a representation. Moving the chair in front of the computer or opening the windows isn't changing *representations*. I don't sit on one either. And my hopes about finding something that has been misplaced aren't for aboutnesses. If they were, presumably we could just *think* our lives better.

Of course, being perceptually conscious involves effects of the objective physical world on you and me. It involves causal and no doubt other lawful connections between the objective physical world and us. Being perceptually conscious involves that world somehow *registering* itself in us, recording itself there, impressing itself, affecting us. But a thing's being somehow registered or whatever doesn't make the registration or lawful correlate into a representation. It doesn't make it into anything like what's in that frame up there on the wall.

So – *what* is actual with you and me now, so far as perceptual consciousness is concerned, is a room, most certainly not a representation of a room, whether called content or anything else whatever – no matter what part representations or things somehow like them play elsewhere, in unconscious mentality, unconscious mentality connected to pieces of conscious mentality.

We can all very well indeed tell the difference between a *sign* of any sort and a thing that isn't one. You know you're not sitting in a representation now, a sign, even if you can start thinking about it in a funny way, maybe as *signifying* something, maybe telling you about yourself.

So, again – perceptual consciousness is not just or even at all *about* that room, but in short *is* only that room. You can only try to say otherwise, it seems to me, by drifting off the subject. If you or I now go a little spiritual or existential, and reflect to ourselves that it's *the place of my life*, that vague but representative reflection isn't at all the real content or object with respect to my now seeing the room – without concentrating on it or on some bit of it or asking something.

Yes, good philosophers have said otherwise about what they take or imply to be ordinary consciousness. Searle, first to be so right about computers and consciousness and all that, says that seeing a car, visual perception, maybe seeing a yellow station wagon, has *in it* a visual experience, a representation of a general sort, which he goes on to define in terms of what he calls its logical features. The representation in perception is of a direct and immediate sort, a presentation, unlike a representation in a belief.

Well, a visual experience sounds like something that is like or is at least along the lines of actual consciousness. But if we understand that, it just isn't the case that what is given along with the yellow station wagon is something else – something, as you can say, that means something else.

Mike Martin once said: 'In being aware of the world, I am aware of my own awareness of it.' Sure, we can be both perceptually and cognitively conscious, of rooms, station wagons and the world. That doesn't get us the conclusion that what is included in what we can call our visual awareness, perceptual consciousness, that kind of actual consciousness, is some kind of consciousness of that consciousness.

You will not really need to hear that what we have here with Searle and Martin seems possibly to be a different subject from ours, or a subject not adequately initially clarified. You know what our subject is. It is hereby assumed that it doesn't leave you in any doubt that being actually conscious in seeing is having something that is not something *about* something else.

More needs to be insisted on here. It's not only representations that are not actual with my perceptual consciousness. Other things are not actual that sure are somehow found there or put into ordinary perceptual consciousness somehow understood in other philosophy and science. This includes items from the five leading ideas other than the first one, qualia, which we've already considered. What is not actual includes something it's like to be something, or a *self* or inner subject, a direction, a kind of experiencing spoken of as phenomenality. And that's still not all that is missing.

When I see my room what is actual doesn't include what is obscurely called a *vehicle* of consciousness as well as what the vehicle conveys – thoughts from my critic McGinn. It doesn't include something called a *medium* of consciousness either, whatever that is. Or something transparent but apparently noticeable or discernible between you and a room. G. E. Moore, who with Russell was the best of Cambridge philosophers, thought he could catch sight of it.

And of course, what is actual with perceptual consciousness doesn't include what you can think of from the theories of consciousness at which we've had a look. In particular, it doesn't include that stock-in-trade of the physicalist theories of which I've reminded you. What is actual with your perceptual consciousness absolutely doesn't ordinarily include your brain or neurons as those are ordinarily and ordinarily scientifically understood. What happens in the life of a surgeon or neuroscientist but not in the lives of the rest of us. And to remember abstract functionalism and traditional dualism, what is actual doesn't itself include causes and effects of what is there, or something somehow unphysical that goes with and supervenes on but isn't the brain or the like.

That's all very well, you may say, but go back to getting rid of representations with perceptual consciousness. You say you've been to a philosophy lecture or two, and you remember what was called the argument from illusion and, what's more, what was called the argument from hallucination. The argument from illusion, as you heard it, was about a bent stick in water. That is what we see. But the stick isn't really bent. It's straight. So what we see is something other than the real thing.

To which can be added by you that trees in the distance look smaller than trees up close. And Tim Crane will remind you very pertinently that if you stick your finger in the corner of your eye, you see differently. That is the beginning of a good run of attempted refutations. There are also at least reflective reminders from Harold Brown in a book edited by Anthony Freeman on a close antecedent of the theory you are considering, then given the name of being *radical externalism*.

There are good replies to all this. One, about the so-called illusions, is that what a real physical stick is, or real tree, is *exactly* something that looks different under different conditions. If it didn't, as was written somewhere, maybe by me, it *wouldn't* be a real physical thing. If a tree didn't look smaller as you got further away from it, it wouldn't be a tree. It would be something like the number 66 or a dream-tree or whatever. God knows what. J. L. Austin, the great adversary in Oxford of A. J. Ayer, was close enough to that proposition, despite far too much commitment to 'ordinary language philosophy'.

And with respect to the hallucinations, real hallucinations, there's also a good reply. In very general terms, it is that what happens in a real hallucination isn't really *like* seeing something at all. There isn't what permits you to figure out that since hallucinating is *like* conscious seeing, therefore seeing must be such and such. Hallucinating is another whole kettle of fish. It's a mystery. It's something along the lines, isn't it, of *thinking you are seeing when you aren't*. This reply is called disjunctivism for reasons we don't have to go into. It calls for your attention in particular to the work of the admirably acute Paul Snowdon of University College London. Another Grote, good successor to Freddie.

So to say it again, what is actual in perceiving is only a *subjective physical world* in the usual sense of a part of the thing. Saying so is comparable to familiar talk of being in touch with the world as ordinarily thought of, or the objective physical world, in virtue of being in touch with a part of it.

But right now something else needs to be added to all the denial of anything else but a room being actual. To leave it out would be unkind or unjust to predecessors and fellow workers, and it would also make for self-doubt about where we are and where we are going.

We began with the five leading and failing ideas of what it was reasonable to suppose was taken as ordinary consciousness by the proponents of the ideas. With the aid of evidence from those proponents we got to a database with respect to ordinary consciousness – took it as actual consciousness. We then looked at various theories of consciousness – at least most of them seeming to be intended as theories of ordinary consciousness.

We have now confidently concluded that what is actual with actual consciousness definitely does not include qualia and the like or the self or more things noted by philosophers whe supplied materials for the database and who offered their own theories of ordinary consciousness. Were they then blunderers who missed out the data they were providing for their superior successors? Blunderers about exactly what is actual in perception?

That is not our line of thinking. Indeed to go in for that line of thinking would be silly. If people ask what is actual with respect to their seeing the room they are in, the answer cannot arguably include qualia or a funny self or whatever. And if our line of thinking included such an imputation that would weaken it.

The facts are different. Our predecessors were operating with something or with several things that they only *indicated*, what we can sum up as *indicated* consciousness. Some did not exclude from it what from our point of view, from the point of view of ordinary and actual consciousness, is *unconscious* mentality. If there is mistaken philosophy there, and no adequate initial clarification of a subject matter, there is no including of qualia and self in *actual* consciousness. These fellow workers were not blunderers.

Are you tempted to a parting shot with respect to all you've now heard about what is actual with perceptual consciousness? Do you say, having thought, that it's obviously true that all that's actual is the room, that there's something of which the only true description is the room, that there's some question to which only the room is the only right answer? But, do you say, *that* just shows I'm not on about the right thing, not giving an answer to the real question, not dealing, really, in some sense of 'really', with what consciousness is?

Well, you had better wait a while before making that judgement. There is more coming to you about perceptual consciousness, quite a lot. And we will of course have to think more in the end, including about whether in going on about ordinary and actual consciousness we have been going on about the right subject, asking the right question.

Maybe right now you feel like another parting shot, anyway your own parting question. Is a subjective physical world just a *phantom* world? Certainly it hasn't been identified as what we

know about, the objective physical world. It's been identified as
not that. So is it insubstantial, imaginary, imagined, dreamed up?
Do you take it that talking of *a room* rather than *the room* is denying the reality or diminishing the reality of the thing? Not just
distinguishing a kind of reality?

If you feel like saying this, and hence if you are are in a good
tradition of philosophical scepticism, you make me feel that I'm
in good company. But hang on for a while. Hold your horses.

Are you, being a philosopher or student who has escaped the
insularities of philosophy in English, also tempted to something
else, a parting question if not a parting shot? Do you ask about or
suspect the existence of a relation or relations to lines of fundamental progress in Continental philosophy? That history of thinking
as inclined to reciprocal condescension of philosophy in English
as philosophy in English is inclined to stand in to it? Do you
mention Edmund Husserl? Martin Heidegger? Jürgen Habermas?
Certainly Jean-Paul Sartre? Maybe Simone de Beauvoir? Maurice
Merleau-Ponty? Others?

You are not alone. You have a companion in the aforemen-
tioned excellent English and Oxford philosopher Stephen Priest,
rational in his admiration of the other side. Make your way to
his critical thinking too on the radical externalism theory of consciousness, a predecessor of the Actualism theory now on offer to
you. See the bibliographies at the end here – the readings for this
particular chapter and also the general readings.

NINE

CONSCIOUSNESS IN SEEING: BEING ACTUAL

There's our second question, the second criterion. What is a room's *being actual*? What does that come to?

Quite a lot – but in sum just its somehow existing, existing in a particular way, it itself somehow existing. Nothing else – its existing, like anything else, in connection with other things, including dependencies on them. Its being actual *is* its existing in an entirely literal sense. Nothing metaphorical or otherwise figurative. Nothing literary either, or metaphysical in any alarming sense, or remote from science, let alone oratorical or flaky.

A room's being actual consists in counterparts to other characteristics we know about, those of the objective physical world. Some of the characteristics of the room are identical with those of the objective physical world's characteristics, some not. Several are more particular. The characteristics of the objective physical world, you'll remember, divided into its physical ones, first, and then objective ones. The characteristics of subjective physical worlds are physical ones and then subjective ones.

This existing of a room, to mention just its most notable characteristics, is its being out there in that space and lasting through some time, and being in two great lawful connections, two dependencies that distinguish this way of existing.

The first dependency is the categorial lawful one on what we know about, *the objective physical world*. In particular the dependency is of stages or space-time parts of a subjective physical world on stages of the objective physical world.

The second dependency with my subjective world is the categorial one on my own objective properties as a perceiver, neural properties and location for a start. The second dependency is on what includes my unconscious mentality, of course neural and of course unconscious in our own sense in this inquiry, which is to say not at all actually conscious. It is a dependency on, in part, effects of the objective physical world out there, registrations that can only mistakenly or misleadingly be called *representations* in another sense of that somewhat loose and somewhat abused word. They are misleadingly so called because they would have to be definitely *unconscious* representations. They are not in either cognitive nor affective consciousness.

Do you ask if something out there can have a necessary condition of its existence in here? Can something out there have a dependency on something in my head? Keep cool, and wait for a while.

You will guess that all this – a subjective physical world, the two dependencies – is true to if certainly not derived only from what you will remember, the two natures or characters of the database, its being both ontic or existential and also epistemic. Put off for a while any idea or worry that we are taking a *leap* at this point *from* something's being actual in the initial sense, that is, from the database and the encapsulation of it as something's being actual, *to* its being subjectively physical, to the theory and analysis. Put off grumbling that it's all very well to think and say the general thing, maybe take the general advice that we need something new in thinking about consciousness, that we need to make a leap to a new theory – but ask what about the particular leap from database to subjective physicality? Is that leap suspect? Despite the ontic and epistemic continuity, I and maybe you have worried or anyway paused for a while about this. Come back to it we will.

Staying with subjective physical worlds now, you may well guess, or not be surprised to hear, that these *subjective worlds* are a vast subset, *the objective physical world* being another sub-set, a one-member subset if a member of many parts, of the single all-inclusive world that there is, *the physical world*, that totality of the things that there are.

By way of digression, this is in fact a third and different and I'd guess much more reasonable answer to something, the question of whether everything whatever that exists is physical or whether it is all mental, conscious or spiritual. That is the question disputed in the old philosophical history of general metaphysics, the dispute between universal materialism or realism and universal philosophical idealism or immaterialism; that question answered so differently by the middle British empiricist so-called, Bishop Berkeley, and also by Hegel and other so-called idealists, as against ancient Greek materialists and such successors as La Mettrie and Holbach and no doubt a lot of working scientists.

About Actualism, if you fancy aphorisms, you may remember Berkeley's summing up of the universal philosophical idealism or spiritualism that he put in place of universal materialism. *Esse est percipi.* To be is to be perceived. There is a better aphorism summing up our Actualism about perceptual consciousness: *To be perceptually conscious is for something in a way to be.*

To say more, my being perceptually conscious now, as something's being actual, is the existence of a stage of a sequence that is one *subjective physical world*, one among very many, as many as there are sets of perceivings of single perceivers. Being conscious in perceiving isn't having representations of whatever sort of an existing thing out there – it's a thing's existing out there.

These myriad worlds, to put it to you again, are no less real for the fact of there being a myriad of them as against the one objective physical world. They are no less real, either, for their stages being more transient than many familiar stages or whatever of *the objective physical world*. Remember that myriad and transient things within the *objective* physical world do not fail to exist on account of being myriad and transient. Science is full of such things.

Speaking of *a* room being actual rather than *the* room, of course, is not at all to diminish it or allow that it is somehow suspect, but mainly just to distinguish it from that other thing, the objective physical room. Subjective physical worlds and their stages, by the way, are in the plain-enough category of states of affairs or circumstances as generally ordinarily understood. They are, we can quickly say, ways that things or objects are, sets of things and properties or relations. They are a long way from what turns up in the philosophical idealism or indeed spiritualism of Bishop Berkeley, although comparison between that idealism and our Actualism could be considered by the acute E. J. Lowe of the acute philosophy department at Durham University.

Subjective physical worlds, even if often fleeting, are about as real as the objective physical world, if differently real. They are about as real in pretty much the sum of decent senses of that loose and wandering word. There are plain reasons, in a list that is coming up, for including the *species* subjective physical worlds along with the *species* objective physical world in the *genus* physical world. They are indeed out there. And, as you will be hearing, subjective physical worlds are dependent on several things, one being the objective physical world.

In one sense, of course, subjective physical worlds are *more* real than the objective physical world – as in effect is often enough remarked. We spend our lives in our subjective physical worlds. But they have their name in this inquiry not because of traditional ideas about subjectivity having to do with a metaphysical self and so on, which you know about, but for better reasons.

One reason is their difference from the objective physical world. Another, connected, is their dependence not only on the objective physical world but on perceivers neurally. Another specific and large reason to which we will come is no funny self but an untraditional fact of subjectivity, the fact of what will also rightly be regarded as individuality or personal identity.

But to get on with introducing Actualism, if by reiteration, you already know from our inquiry into *what* is actual with perceptual consciousness that my being perceptually conscious is *only* a particular existence of something like or related to what most or all of the leading ideas and the previous theories of consciousness take perceptual consciousness merely to be *of* or *about* or *to represent*.

There is also that other difference – the leading ideas and the theories take perceptual consciousness to be a lot more than just a represented room or whatever. There's the vehicle, the medium, the transparent what-not, and whatever else.

One last proposition of introduction to subjective physical worlds. In talking of them, we're not discovering an entirely new thing, a new category. This isn't construction, let alone invention out of thin air. Instead, however *we* got here, we're noting and using and not being distracted from an old thing, putting it into a theory of perceptual consciousness, making a theory from it and necessarily leaving other stuff out. That is, there certainly has been talk and theory in the past of some or other physical world *being there for us*, in the ordinary sense of a part of it being there. There's been talk of *the world as experienced*. It's the stuff of more than philosophy.

Also strengths of German and French and other Continental philosophy as against what is often called Analytic philosophy, certainly strengths not enough known about by me, to say the least in place of my further embarrassment. There is Heidegger on conceptions of the world and indeed worlds, and on consciousness as being a different ontological category from that of the objective physical world. There is his difference with respect to mental images and other representations in perceptual consciousness.

There are Sartre's dramatic departures from Anglo-Saxon thinking, certainly newness in philosophy, but departures that include some intersections if not affinities with what we have been thinking about perceptual consciousness. Maybe a likeness despite difference with respect to a matter we will get to the in the end, the relation of consciousness and our human freedom.

But leave all that. There's a subjective physical world for you right now, isn't there? You're immediately in touch with one of those right now, aren't you? If this familiar fact doesn't by itself give you a step to Actualism with respect to perceptual consciousness, it's a very helpful pull in the right direction.

Now the nitty-gritty, being pedestrian again. A checklist of characteristics of subjective physical worlds. As already remarked, first physical characteristics, then subjective.

Physical Characteristics

Are subjective *physical* worlds such that there must be significant hesitation about regarding perceptual consciousness as consisting in them? As earlier with our consideration of objective physical worlds, wait until the end here for an answer.

(1) Subjective physical worlds, about as much as the objective physical world and perceivers, are within the inventory or taxonomy of present and anticipated psychology, neuroscience and other science. It matters not at all that those sciences have not made much or even any use of our conception of subjective physical worlds in investigating the fact of perception. It does not matter that they have at least tended to mislocate consciousness – tended mistakenly to internalize it. It does not matter that they have at least concentrated on the internal lawful condition of consciousness, taking it as the thing itself. We can say for ourselves, as implied already, that to focus attention on something, use it in a theory, use it in answering a question, is hardly ever to discover what was never heard of. Using what somehow has been accepted has more to be said for it than invention.

Philosophers have often been barefaced enough to be ready enough to try to be little Copernicuses, but it is to be noted that even Copernicus's real revolution did not at all get rid of all previous astronomy. Seeing things differently, seeing the relation of the earth to the sun differently, did not get rid of anything like all of what had been found out about those things. So with Actualism.

(2) As certainly it is the case that subjective physical worlds, perceivers and the objective physical world are within the method or methods of psychology, neuroscience and other science. The qualifications having to do with differences between subjective physicality, perceivers and objective physicality, say with respect to measurement, do not much affect the proposition.

To look at something differently, obviously, to say it again, is not necessarily to subtract it from earlier investigation. Indeed, since Actualism is thinking about facts rather than getting them, which line of life is certainly not identical with scientific method, it would be very surprising if the theory was not within what is open to scientific method.

(3) That subjective physical worlds, perceivers and the objective physical world are in space and time is as indubitable. Anyway as indubitable as is possible with one of the three being not only familiar but in a way novel.

Has *anyone* mistakenly supposed that other philosophers and scientists, not yet converted to Actualism, have spoken of a perceived world and also spoken yet more informally of such a thing, and taken it to be *nowhere* and of *no* duration in time? How could it be, incidentally, that things within perceived worlds or subjective physical worlds, say chairs and pieces of paper, are within space and time, often in the wrong places, without whatever contains them being so? And you are reminded that you can *measure* in your world, and use your watch.

(4) There is no doubt about things within subjective physical worlds being in causal and other lawful connections than there is about things in the objective physical world being in such connections. Indeed, given the fact of the actuality of the more numerous worlds, there is less doubt about lawful connections. Despite certain interpretations of quantum theory, my coffee cup never elevates itself. The world we all live in, presumably connected to what's down below, *never* confirms indeterminism, *never* confirms absolute inexplicableness. That's a very big fact. Is there a bigger one?

(5) Evidently there are lawful connections between the categories that are subjective physical worlds and the two categories that are the objective physical world out there and the neural categories of perceivers. There is no more reason to doubt this than that there was doubt in the old days about lawful connection between the brain and supervening consciousness.

(6) One of two characterizations of subjective physical worlds as having to do with perception is exactly what we are taking to be the fundamental truth about perceptual consciousness: that is, that the existence of subjective physical worlds just *is* the fact of the objective physical world being perceived, that fact as we ordinarily and unreflectively speak of it.

(7) Another characterization having to do with perception is that things in a subjective physical world are perceived from different points of view – as are things in the case of the objective physical world.

(8) So a thing in a subjective physical world is different from different points of view. Both this proposition and (7) and others, of course, bear on the mistake that a subjective physical world is something in the head or a phantom world or whatever.

(9) The properties of things in subjective physical worlds include both primary and secondary properties – the second category necessarily not distinguished by the dependence on perceivers that in our Actualism is shared with primary properties, a dependence with all perception. Rather, for present purposes, secondary properties can be identified by enumeration – as being those of colour, sound, warmth and cold, and taste, and not shape, size, motion, solidity and number.

Yes, there must be a question of a special dependency on perceivers of our secondary properties. Here is a particular case of Actualism opening a question worth answering, giving rise to rather than being a dead end in inquiry. Are there larger cases?

Subjective Characteristics

(10) Subjective physical worlds are subjective in that they cannot conceivably be separate from consciousness for various

reasons, one being that they *are* the existence of perceptual consciousness.

(11) A subjective physical world is to an extent private. It is in practice the perceptual consciousness of only one particular perceiver.

(12) Each subjective physical world is at least in practice a matter of some extent of privileged access by the perceiver, a greater confidence, certainly not infallibility or incorrigibility.

(13) Our beliefs and judgements with respect to subjective physical things may be taken to be less governed by the pursuit of factual truth and logic than judgements with objective physical things are or are presumed to be.

(14) If subjective physical properties raise particular problems for scientific method, clearly they are not beyond it.

(15) To anticipate something of large importance to which we will eventually come, your subjective physical world is a great component of the particular fact of subjectivity that is your individuality. This is no eerie self or the like, but a unity over time owed to and indeed united by dependencies and interdependencies of lawfulness and meaning. It is a unity containing cognitive and affective consciousness and more of the mental than that. Its full description will include ideas of physical as distinct from abstract functionalism.

(16) To revert now to that question touched on at the start, the above properties of subjective physical worlds, in contrast to objective physical properties and despite that thinking about zombies, are *not* good cause for hesitancy about consciousness consisting in them.

With respect to the list, I first repeat that philosophy does not have large proofs in it. That was learned early by me from a line of teachers I was lucky to have had – Ayer, Hampshire, Watling,

Williams, Wollheim. Philosophy has weights of argument – which may leave alternatives open. It is possible that the list of characteristics can be improved, as the list of characteristics of the objective physical world could have been improved. But surely an improved list of characteristics of the objective physical would have allowed for a like transition to characteristics of the subjective physical worlds.

If you share my attitude to philosophy in connection with the impossibility of large proofs, a realism about philosophy itself, you will not for a moment expect that questions will not arise with respect to Actualism on perceptual consciousness and in particular the above characteristics. You will have at least felt the possibility of questions. So have I, God knows.

But Actualism is a theory different enough, enough of a departure from those five leading ideas and the many existing theories of consciousness, to make the main business in this book, as indeed it was of its big brother, necessarily the laying out of the main thing for early visitors rather than thinking as much about responses to it. Trying to make something stand up comes before reinforcing and defending it, not to mention freeing doors and filling cracks.

I worry that someone said to Professor Quine of Harvard after a lecture there by Professor Popper that Professor Popper lectured with a broad brush, to which Professor Quine mused in reply that maybe he thought with one too.

Anyway with perceptual consciousness now little more can be done than indicate the questions by labelling them and then indicating my own present responses to them, usually very briefly.

Circularity? You may remember my declarative denial of an imputation against the database – that it, like the five leading ideas and more, is open to the objection of circularity. Denied it still is, but now add something else, about what we have now. There is no conceivable possibility of taking the theory or analysis of what it is to be conscious of the place you're in to be circular. There's *far* too much there for a start.

The surprise of this externalism? Actualism at least goes well beyond the seemingly universal but particular externalisms of Putnam, Burge, Noë and Clark. Yes, it's a lot more radical. It's a different ball game. Yes, it's stranger, just strange. All those externalisms, despite Putnam's having changed his mind about where meanings ain't, call out for the attention of the assiduous student – even if they all may take perceptual consciousness merely to be *of* or *about* a room, not our specified existence of a room. But they aren't what we're thinking about.

But my point right now is that the customariness of internalism or cranialism about consciousness can be no big deal. All you can philosophically honourably do is consider lines of argument. And you are reminded that Dr Johnson was endearing in refuting Berkeley by kicking a stone, but also a bit of an ass. Whatever yen you have for an old internalism about consciousness, it's possible to hope that you now have as strong a one to a theory that includes an externalism.

Consensus? There is more of a problem, probably, about something connected with externalism. That is its being a case of going against what has some claim to being the consensus of a profession, going against the fellow workers mentioned a few times. Well, small excuses or anyway remarks hurry to mind. How clear and large is the consensus of internalism? There is or was that externalist quartet. They didn't have trouble getting published.

And there is what should have got more time from me in the past, a certain philosophical tradition, that of *naive realism*, so named by its adversary Freddie Ayer, now sometimes called *direct realism.* As remarked earlier, it is somehow to the effect that in perception we're in some unexplained direct relation to the *objective* physical world. It has gone right on inchoately outside philosophy and lately been renamed *direct realism* and found a definitely sophisticated kind of friend inside philosophy – Mike Martin, formidable former colleague already mentioned and now Californian professor as well.

Bravely, and just making up the opportunity in passing, it needs to be confessed that a more completely diligent tour-guide than me, on a better class of tour, say like a Swan Hellenic one of the Aegean and Ionian seas, would detain you now about something, or would have detained you earlier, maybe in that bird's-eye view of theories of consciousness.

We would indeed have paused before the work of Mike in seeking to save naive realism from its past, even despite his included proposition that 'In being aware of the world, I am aware of my own awareness of it.' There is the additional reason that he refers to his view as being an Actualism. Rise above your guide. Go to the Readings. Do not join me in the elderly habit of waiting for the book.

Two last remarks about respecting consensus. Philosophically honourably, you can't stay in philosophy and also give up on the occupational concentration on just clarity, consistency and validity, completeness and generalness. That doesn't include sucking up. Also relevant to any claim of consensus, remember those declarations of the need for something new about consciousness.

Unbelievability? Now to go forward with respect to our Actualism, the genuine article, what about the response to it of unbelievability? Actualism had to clarify itself further in the past to resist responses of unbelievability. McGinn, despite his demand for the new, was more than shocked by early papers on it, as remarked already. It has now made more of an escape from being unbelievable. And there is more escaping to come here.

Real physicality? You will not, it is hoped, put to me the question of whether subjective physical worlds are *really* physical or not. You should be alive to the ambiguity and so on of 'real' and 'really'. And consider again the division of the physical in general into objective and subjective physicalities, and the clarifications of them. And yes, incidentally, since somebody asked, I take it that subjective physical worlds have mass, in a way different from but of course related to the mass of the objective physical world.

A baroque theory? It's been said by Derek Matravers that Actualism is that. But *is* Actualism about perceptual consciousness on the way to being complex and extravagant? Surely not. It is just not as misleadingly simple as alternatives. If the problem of consciousness was simple, it would have been put to rest quite a while ago, wouldn't it?

And is Actualism out of sight of ordinary informed and reflective belief and talk? Don't forget the world as experienced, being there for us and so on. Action at a distance? On account of the internal necessary condition of subjective physical worlds? Is Actualism to be charged with this – if that is the right verb? Don't know. Not if action at a distance is residually spooky. I don't like the sound of it at all if it puts some constraint on possible kinds of lawful connection. Presumably there are or can be causal pairs not involving intermediaries.

Multiplication of reality? A theory containing *two* worlds, *two* desks, one objectively physical and one subjectively physical. And containing a stage of a subjective physical room *going missing* when you leave. Its not existing any longer. Do I have the face to say so? Yes, for reasons explained. Why not two worlds and desks? And why not the proposition of a stage going missing? – don't forget it is certain to be replaced by a similar one when you come back upstairs, maybe qualitatively identical or near enough.

Newton said, let nature speak for itself – whatever it says. Nature including us. So too with good argument about nature. Keep on trying to hang on to it. To accept a line of argument, you are reminded, must be to try to put up contentedly with questions as jibes. Do succeed.

Ontology and epistemology? Is it confusion to mix up ontology with epistemology, as in the database and then the theory of perceptual consciousness? The mix *does* turn up in the database. There are those facts. The mix isn't just another good idea.

Relations of the kinds of properties? Is there room for more thought about the relation of objective physical properties to subjective physical properties? You bet – and in my anticipation, without disaster.

Relations of meaning? Are they to be added to relations of lawfulness in thinking more about Actualism? Could be. Think about it. Maybe write something.

The science of perception and subjective physical worlds? The science is at least consistent with what you have heard. Actualism also a reassurance to science? It makes perceptual consciousness clear, real, different.

That easy rhetoric about 'two kinds of world'? Not respectable? Too pop? Anyway pop? Suspect? No doubt more restrained or technical or other language could have been used. With no headline on it. I plead a little guilty, as a lot of scientists have to about their theories and results. But don't forget that there is the story under the headline of two kinds of worlds. You heard it. It exists. There are those literal lists of characteristics.

A zombie? Do you suppose that all that has been said so far of a particular thing could be true – there could be, with respect to it, a stage of a subjective physical world with the two dependencies and so on – and the particular thing could be not ordinarily perceptually conscious at all? Just a zombie in that sense? I've wondered, of course, having looked at the pages of Robert Kirk of Nottingham and also Chalmers.

And then I've become confident that the question is a case of illusion, maybe a shared illusion. Call it the more-to-consciousness illusion. God knows there are shared illusions. One about democracy and equality for a start. Consciousness, you may agree, is just the subject or place for one. And there is more to say about what somebody thinks could not be ordinarily conscious at all. There is more to say, for instance, about individuality.

Strangeness? There's more to say about it than you heard about above with surprisingness. That question in objection to Actualism about perceptual consciousness, *although understandable*, makes diametrically the wrong use of a strong proposition.

Consciousness, as soon as you start thinking about it, *is* strange. It *is* unusual, something else, a little eerie itself, at least unsettling, certainly absolutely unique. It calls out for an account that is not humdrum, not in sight of humdrum. Nor is this unknown with other subjects, unknown in other subjects than philosophy. Go back once more to that encyclopaedia of science. We too need a theory that *saves* strangeness.

The affront of it all? There's a general point to be made about a lot of those related objections – the surprise of a real externalism, going against consensus, unbelievability, baroqueness, multiplication of reality, easy rhetoric about worlds and strangeness. All of that mainly or primarily about Actualism on perceptual consciousness. Much of it pressed or implied by an early anonymous reader of the manuscript of this book.

As I say, there's a general point in reply. Compare Actualism with representative or sense-data theories of perception, general theories of consciousness that make no big difference of perceptual consciousness against cognitive and affective, objective physicalisms, traditional dualism and abstract functionalism, anomalous monism, aspectural theories, quantum theory consciousness, the union theory and more. There's the possibility of our arguing that Actualism is *less* remote from common sense and so on, gives *less* affront than the competing theories.

Old hat? Do you now unkindly change your whole tune? Do you wonder instead if Actualism about perceptual consciousness is somehow just old hat? What you may have in mind, maybe, is that tradition of naive or direct realism. But Actualism is well out of sight of that. The tradition, surely, has been just or hardly more than a denial of sense data and all that, hardly more than a denial, however welcome, of the idea of our always seeing reality on inner television, as Fred Dretske so memorably remarked of representative theories of perception.

The tradition of naive realism, it seems, has merely been to the effect that in perception we're in some unexplained direct relation to the *objective* physical world. Actualism is certainly different. It comes from that database for a start. It goes on from there. There's so much more to it. You don't have to be brave to say it *explains*.

Could it be that Actualism transforms but thereby preserves the intuitive and maybe atavistic conviction of naive realism with perceptual consciousness, the idea that persisted against the inner stuff of Locke, Berkeley and Hume since their centuries? It's possible to hope so, as I've recently started to do.

Do you half-wonder if Actualism is another kind of old hat, more often worn? Is it just the refrain that perceptual experience includes a *content* and *something else*, a container, vehicle, some kind of directedness, being-about, presentation or what-not? To really think that, you would have to have nodded off in our relationship for quite a while. In brief, Actualism is that being perceptually conscious is a dependent existence of a world, which fact includes no container, presenter or anything of the sort – of, as you will not have forgotten, any representation in a more familiar sense.

Supervenience? Does that old problem of the connection of consciousness and brain remain on your mind? Well, with perceptual consiousness, we now have a different landscape – our perceptual consciousness being a subjective physical world dependent on *both* objective world and brain. To go back to Davidson, it was never really clear to me why he supposed there could not be psychophysical laws.

Mysterianism? In my view, as you know, goodbye to all that. We have perfectly intelligible connection between consciousness and what it depends on – we have ordinary lawful connection. Hard to disdain, the very stuff of science. And more such connection to come with cognitive and affective consciousness.

Yes, the mighty McGinn disdained just lawful connection as being 'brute correlation', not something somehow more 'explanatory'. My own response includes my seemingly greater respect for science, for explained lawfulness and for its issue in more questions of lawful connection. That progress and related progress. Also what *is* the supposed higher intelligibility? I rather like lower myself.

Difference of consciousness? This fact of consciousness has been first of all a demand for an account of consciousness making it not objectively physical. We have such an account for perceptual consciousness. We also have more than that. For a large start, an account of a side of consciousness, the perceptual side, that is, externalism without representationism.

Fertile theory? Yes of course, with respect to both philosophical and scentific work in the theory itself. It is indeed a workplace. Say with perceptual vis-à-vis affective consciousness. Also fertile or useful elsewhere, outside the theory? You can think or guess so. Contemplate for an instant an explanatory contribution to the problem of the nature of truth. A contribution to the realism that is a form of the compelling theory of truth – to the effect that truth is correspondence to fact.

In terrible quickness here, Actualism makes fundamental fact *integral* to perceptual consciousness itself, not fundamental fact in need of some linkage to consciousness that brings in another statement and hence something like the coherence theory of truth.

All of these are questions and indications of answers with respect to Actualism as we have it so far. As you know, there is more of it to come. That is the part with respect to cognitive and affective consciousness. Like what we have, this will include a new thing or two.

Does novelty already and the prospect of more of it make you uncertain? Reflect on the opinion of Paul Grice, a clever English philosopher gone to ground in California. 'My taste for keeping an open house for all sorts and conditions of entities, just so long as when they come in they help with the house-work. Provided that I can see them at work, and provided that they are not detected in illicit logical behaviour . . . I do not find them queer or mysterious at all. To fangle a new ontological Marxism, they work therefore they exist.'

Yes, it seems, Actualism as we have it so far works, is licit, isn't really queer. As for illicit, there are those other theories of perceptual consciousness that make it all about representation. It isn't. You know too that those theories – even the previous externalist theories to an extent – put perceptual consciousness in a head. It isn't in there. It is a state of affairs, more of which is outside of a head.

Finally, it comes to me today, for the first time, that you may be pesky to the end, mutter a certain charge. This Actualism, you mutter or even say, is *metaphysics*.

Being a proper philosopher, if very smallish as against figures in the history of the subject, I can pretend no superiority to a main part of metaphysics, or what is known of of it by me. Say a little Kant, necessarily something of our three empiricists Locke, Berkeley and Hume, a little of Peter van Inwagen, something of Strawsons Sr and Jr. Rather than pretend superiority, admit the fault I do of no conscious work in or with metaphysics. Would that a scientist or two, including one who in living memory announced in the newspapers that philosophy is dead, had something like that rational attitude.

Abstention is my obligation with respect to adding in any general way to the general negative commentary on metaphysics in its variations – defensively grandiose, pious, respectful, philosophically self-certifying, insecure, condescendingly critical, necessarily ignorant and so on. What is needed here is mainly just a reminder.

Call it whatever else you want, but what we have been engaged in is just standard philosophy. As you'll remember, just that greater concentration than that of science on the logic of ordinary intelligence – (a) clarity, usually analysis, (b) consistency and validity, (c) completeness, (d) generalness.

Where we are at the moment is that your being conscious in seeing the room consists in a room's, your room's, being there and being dependent on the objective physical world, a stage of it, and dependent on you objectively physically, you neurally and perceptually. That is the theory or analysis or understanding of a room's being actual, that fact within your perceiving the room. You'll remember that 'the room' is being used to refer to the objectively physical thing and 'a room' to refer to the subjectively physical thing.

We also want and need language for this whole fact of your being perceptually conscious, and what is most natural is speaking of the state of affairs or circumstance that is the existing of something dependent on two other things. A state of affairs does indeed have a location – the location of the three things of which it is comprised.

On reflection, surely, you are under no temptation to say it is nowhere. You do not for a moment suppose that the state of affairs of a flower's opening or being open is nowhere? Or that a seduction was nowhere? Or a war? Or a dying? You do not for a moment suppose that the state of affairs of your being perceptually conscious is missing from space and time. How could it be?

And of course we have language to express the fact. Your being conscious in seeing the room is a state of affairs or an event, very generally speaking – a *thing or things* having *a property or properties* or being in a *relation or relations* for a time. That, we can agree, is just what your being conscious in seeing the room is a case of.

When you think more of that, however, you will be inclined to find or make a difference between (i) the existings of the three things – a room, the room, you – and (ii) the existence of the whole state of affairs, including the relationships. You may in plain and pretty useless English be inclined to say each of the three things is *more there* than the state of affairs is *there*. That first step is not to subtract the state of affairs from space and time, of course. How could we? California and Somerset are states of affairs.

But there is thinking and judging and deciding to be done, distinguishing – in fact philosophy on exactly states of affairs. Quite a lot relevant to this has been done already. For a start have a look at that admirable online resource *The Stanford Encyclopedia of Philosophy*. Put 'relations' into the box and spend some time with the articles on 'Properties', 'David Lewis's Metaphysics' and 'Medieval Theories of Relations'. The questions have a recent as well as a long history. They cannot be the stuff of our thinking together today. Any more than any philosophy on anything can have in it the stuff of all that comes up in it, starting with truth in it. But there are two or three certainties. One is that there exist states of affairs or circumstances or things having properties or being in relations. A second is that they are where they are – where the composing or possessing or related things are.

The third is that Actualism, as you have heard already, insofar as it has to do with perceptual consciousness and in more than that, is not a finished theory. Rather, no doubt like almost all decent theories, it issues in more questions. It *is* indeed fertile, pregnant or, as the philosopher of science Imre Lakatos at the London School of Economics with some politics in his past used to say, progressive rather than degenerating.

One more idea here. You have heard my proposition that the problem of consciousness, so much disagreement, has significantly been owed to no single question being asked. Is there another smaller but also significant source? That is, problems within the problem of consciousness. One of those is the general one of those states of affairs, the wide category that has in it your being conscious of the room you're in. We always knew consciousness isn't *stuff*, but we weren't perfectly clear about states of affairs and the like.

So Actualism, you may agree, is fertile with respect not only to science but to philosophy. You may also agree that what you have heard of Actualism and will be hearing is not put in doubt by the arising questions. Any such general attitude would be no less than the cancellation of science and philosophy, not to mention a lot else, like trying to think what is right by and in societies.

TEN

THINKING AND WANTING:
WHAT IS ACTUAL?

We turn from perceptual consciousness to the second and the third sides of consciousness – these second and third subjects taken together.

What is actual with your cognitive consciousness? Say your remembering your sister when she was young, or contemplating that there are different physicalities, or asking some question, or attending to something in the room you're perceptually conscious of? And what is actual with the third side of consciousness, the affective? Are you feeling OK, confident, fancying a cup of coffee, maybe intending to get one soon?

In the history of the philosophy and science of mind, there have been three more or less distinguishable large problems: the mind–body problem, the problem of perception and, latterly, the main problem of consciousness. The last one has been the problem to which responses have included those five leading ideas of consciousness with which we began, qualia to phenomenality, and then the subsequent range of theories or analyses of consciousness – dualism, abstract functionalism, supervenience, anomalous monism, union theory, mentalism, naturalism, aspectualisms, particular physicalisms, higher-order thought theory, eliminative materialism, first-person point of view, quantum consciousness, and the four seemingly universal but particular externalisms, of meanings ain't in the head, arthritis in the thigh, minds extending to maps, consciousness *as* acting.

In considerations of the three large problems, even the mind–body problem and the problem of perception, there has to my knowledge been no concern with the proposition that there are large differences in exactly consciousness, differences *in* what it itself is, differences that have to be included in an effective general or summative account of it. Differences *between* the three sides of consciousness – consciousness in seeing and other perceiving, and consciousness as thinking and as wanting. What there has been instead is the assuming, formulating or defending of *universal and uniform* ideas or theories. As you have heard a couple of times, flattened theories.

This has indeed been the case with the mind–body problem, of which the source or root or impetus has in fact surely been the third and larger problem of the nature of consciousness. It has been close enough to true that universal and uniform theories of consciousness have been the case even with the problem of perception – at bottom disagreement between the tradition of naive realism and the like as against the tradition of inner sense data and the rest. In naive realism the role given to external realities has in fact not made for change or distinction with respect to perceptual consciousness itself as against cognitive and affective. There has been no such clarity.

The same goes for the five leading ideas and with the theories enumerated for the free-standing problem of consciousness. There is, finally, the same or a close enough fact of uniformity with concern with incidental problems of consciousness, for example the special subject of privileged access and maybe the special fact of attending to something in consciousness in perceiving.

Was this assumption of there being a universal and uniform answer to the question of the nature of consciousness itself right? Is the right answer to the question of the nature of consciousness really single or Procrustean? Has such an assumption been owed to no adequate initial clarification of the subject matter of consciousness – and hence in particular to no concern with actual consciousness? Has the assumption been owed to lesser facts as well? Maybe, surprisingly, owed to a mixing up of perceptual consciousness with the obviously different fact of attending to something in it?

Well, we ourselves settled an adequate initial clarification. Being conscious is something's being actual. If actual consciousness is our subject, is it the case that we too, in pressing on with an analysis of consciousness, a theory of its nature, will come to a uniform and universal answer? The same kind of flat answer with respect to all of perceptual, cognitive and affective consciousness? No. Definitely not. What is actual now with your seeing, hearing and touching, as we have already concluded, is a subjective physical world – a room, things in it. That is what is given, had, not deduced or the like, and so on.

What about cognitive and affective consciousness? Well, a natural answer in its most general form is that what is actual is ideas, or to speak more usefully, *representations* or *aboutnesses*. Is that answer right? If so, definitely, given the difference from percepual consciousness, there is no uniform and universal answer to the question of what all consciousness is.

There is a second question, seemingly harder, whose fullest consideration will be delayed for the next phase of all this. If we do proceed in terms of representations or aboutnesses with cognitive and affective consciousness, shall we join a lot of philosophers and scientists in taking or assuming or seeming to take cognitive and affective consciousness as consisting *only* in representations, *purely* or *exclusively* in representations? That is commonly at least implied.

With respect to the first question, of what is actual, yes, it is at least natural to give the general answer that what is actual is indeed representations, in some sense or other. Perhaps all of the uniform and universal theories of consciousness, whatever their exact questions, have been on their strongest ground in their policy that thinking and wanting in their various forms, as against consciousness in perceiving, are somehow a matter of representations. In doing this, they have of course taken representations as essentially being a matter of two-term or dyadic relations, relations between the representation and the represented thing.

With all or nearly all or most of the five leading consciousness ideas and then the theories, there is not only inclusion of representations, but the tacit assumption, aided by the ambiguity and other vagueness of 'representation', that all consciousness *is* only representations, *is* purely or exclusively representations. All events and states of consciousness consist just in representations, at least typically including implicitly the attitudes having to do with truth and good.

To get on with our own inquiry now, certainly many or most conscious representations are *like* or are somehow related to linguistic representations – those spoken or written representations in ordinary language. With the latter, maybe it is enough to keep in mind (i) names and other referring expressions, (ii) the simple predications that are linkings or concatenations of referring expressions with predicates – say noun phrase and verb phrase, and (iii) such things together with attitudes having to do with either fact or value – these combinations being propositional attitudes.

The study, classification and clarification of linguistic representations, in particular the propositional attitudes, evidently makes for a resource that contributes effectively to understanding what is like or is somehow to be understood by way of those linguistic expressions – cognitive and affective consciousness. So too is there aid in stages of subjective physical worlds and also in images in them, say drawings, both of which exist in relation to mental images, those once-suspect things so admirably defended by the realistic free-thinker already mentioned, Hannay. If word-like as against image-like representations can seem to have a greater role in consciousness, it would be rash indeed to reject a degree and kind of understanding of conscious representation based on ordinary external images.

A word on representations related to truth, representations presented as somehow related to truth. They do, of course, raise the philosophical question of the nature of truth. In my own view, mentioned a long way back, the inescapable correspondence theory of the nature of truth is first to the effect that what we can call foundational statements are true when *what is referred to is as described*. And, secondly, with the rest of statements, existential or general statements for a start, they are true when they stand in the right relations to true foundational statements. 'There are lions' or 'Lions exist' is true when 'That's a lion' is somewhere true, somewhere such that what is referred to is as described.

With respect not to cognitive but to affective consciousness, the representations stand in some connection with what is somehow good, maybe what you can better call an attitude of *wanting* in the generic sense – where wanting and the like includes passions, desires, emotions, valuing, moods, deciding, intending, experiencing in acting and more.

By way of a general characterization, with these latter representations having to do with what is somehow desirable, the aim, as has been said, is having the world closer to fitting the representations, changing or preserving the world – as distinct from with the other representations, concerned with truth, where the aim is having the representations fit the world.

There may be a principle of right and wrong involved in affective consciousness, say the Principle of Humanity. Aesthetic feelings are also stuff of affective consciousness. Think of the beauty of passages of Schubert's *Die schöne Müllerin* – beauty, by the way, not requiring knowledge of the German language.

So, again – there is the general proposition that what is actual, a thought or feeling, is at bottom what is *about* something, in such a sense *of* something. What is actual, an idea or line of inquiry or argument, or a bit of one, or confidence or doubt that something is right or fine or worth having, is not itself just a thing or object, as in the case of perceptual consciousness, but is a thing *about* another thing.

Still, you may join me in wondering if the thing or whatever about which the thought or feeling is – if that is in another way in the story. Not just in the story in that the thought or feeling is about it, and certainly not *there* in the way a room is there in seeing it. How what something is about *is* there in another sense than being represented may be a pretty question worth puzzling about. But over to you. All yours.

If there has been existing philosophical and scientific theory with respect to perceptual consciousness, often consciousness in seeing, recently there has been still more, an awful lot, with respect to cognitive and affective consciousness. At least much of it tries to fill out beginnings of answers with respect to the natures of cognitive and affective consciousness. What is now to be mentioned to you, enough to be getting on with, is little more than a short mixed list, four theories or subjects – with just a comment or two added.

The four have to do with an alleged shared human language you may not have heard of, and a use of the theory of evolution, and relationism or computerism, and lingualism or general philosophy of language applied to the subject of mind. To them is added something on what you may well have heard of, to which we are coming, the Chinese Room thought experiment or argument.

With the things in thinking and wanting, as you have heard, ordinary language comes to mind as a means or aid to their description – ordinary external language such as the one you are reading, English. But one of Jerry Fodor's notable contributions to the study of thinking and wanting is the hypothesis of the *language of thought*, also known as mental language or mentalese.

You are left to look into LOT, as it is abbreviated, in your own study-time, but keep in mind the truistic urging that there are other relevant languages of thought, one being nothing other than English. They are of a different but perhaps as great a use as any such generic language as LOT – for which, by the way, it seems we have not been informed of a settled vocabulary and structure.

For the present we also pass by what is at least as well known, Fodor's well-known lines of despair mentioned earlier about understanding, maybe getting a further or real understanding, of representation or aboutness itself. Finding out *what* it is if it's real.

To the theory of LOT can be added a second theory or subject taken to fill in some or all of the proposition that what is actual with cognitive and affective consciousnesses is representations. This theory or subject is evolutionary causalism, also known as biosemantics and as teleological semantics. Ruth Garrett Millikan and David Papineau. The theory, itself not easy to get into view, or anyway into a brief report, seems to have in its past, remarkably, some philosopher or scientist's very simple idea that representations are to be understood just as effects of what they represent, maybe anyway essentially as effects of what they represent.

The idea is taken to fail for the smallish reason among others of the possibility of a conceivable if certainly rare effect. That is somebody's use of a term, quite mistaken, and maybe disastrous for somebody else, but a use that nevertheless *is* now the effect of what it does *not* represent. Say a very mistaken use now of the term 'donkey' in an intended warning – but in fact a use of the term that is really being caused by a lurking tiger mistakenly seen as a donkey.

Such a difficulty is taken to be escaped by the doctrine that our representations are only for a start things somehow caused by things they represent, caused by what they are about. Crucially they must also be representations of more survival-value for us, more biological advantage, more evolutionary advantage, than certain conceivable 'disjunctive' representations. The latter disjunctive representations are owed not to one kind of past beginning but two, say to the causes in fact being donkeys *or* tigers.

There are various puzzles and questions and objections with respect to this rather elusive doctrine, notably the simple truth that there are standard evolutionary effects, of course most of them, that simply are not representations – say, being tall or blonde. Representations being the right kind of evolutionary effects would not begin to give us a full or anyway much account of what they are, distinguish them. But excused we are from further reflection.

Is there a clearer or more accessible philosophical or scientific theory or subject that aids understanding of thinking and wanting? Something else does call for examination. It is the industry that abstract functionalism about representations has grown into, *relationism*, a physical functionalism that you may also call *computerism*. It is that representations are objective physical intermediaries, certainly not merely abstract, that are also conventional semantic and syntactic signs, and so are connected by meaning as well as causation. It's hard to believe that relationism or computerism has ever been a clear-headed and sufficient answer to a clear question about just consciousness, say anything like actual consciousness. Mentality, all of mentality, would evidently make for a better subject, maybe lead towards a better general answer about representation.

There's also a larger question for us. The whole content of the theory or subject of relationism or computerism is fully exemplified by something simple – a printed line, a sentence, on a page. Say that very sentence. That's something that has well-known representational properties, in particular semantic properties. Say conventions or rules attached to it. The printed line is all that when it is just sitting there, unread, whatever might be said of it when it's being read. So there has to be at least a question, doesn't there, of how far relationism, the philosophy and science of it, just that, gives us the full story of cognitive and affective consciousness. There has to be something more to consciousness, something great I'd say.

You may join me in declaring, however, that relationism or computerism must or anyway may be a new lode of fact for the enrichment of the theory of cognitive and affective consciousness to which we are on the way. Relationism or computerism is such despite the run of objections in the large book of mine that preceded this one, that large book for a fortitudinous reader.

Another possible enrichment of our reflection on cognitive and affective consciousness, after LOT, evolutionary causalism and relationism or computerism, is the whole subject you can call *lingualism*, by which is meant general philosophy of language made good use of in the philosophy of mind. Here Searle's contribution has been great. It is a contribution that issues in a large question.

Does this philosophy of language settle for us or anyway crucially enlighten the philosophy of consciousness? We have already tended in that direction, made some use of lingualism, say in connection with the two kinds of attitudes and the world. Is it of more use? There can be doubt as to how far we can get. Can we get to the end, or anyway get to the end in view – a satisfactorily complete account of cognitive and affective consciousness, of what it is?

Let us press on with our own business. To our answer that *what* is actual with cognitive and affective consciousness is representations is to be added the further proposition that nothing else is actual. Certainly the same things that turn up in other consciousness theories are as absent here as they were with perceptual consciousness. A metaphysical self is missing – whatever has to be supplied in the end with respect to the conviction that consciousness has something at least important to do with talk of subjectivity, something that is the real content of the talk. But let that wait.

We have not looked into a lot. We have not for ourselves looked into the coming into being of representations, let alone all of what using them comes to. Say the naming of children and the use of the names. You don't have to be Einstein. And thus a look at representing as being a special exercise of *memory*, and maybe best or anyway well studied within that narrower subject within consciousness. More promising than help from evolution? You can certainly suspect we have not got enough of the nature of conscious representations in general by speaking of them just as aboutnesses or as things meaning other things.

Only one known question hereabouts can be mentioned. How can and does a representation represent, how can and does a word *mean*, something that doesn't exist at all – say the fountain of youth or Bertrand Russell's *the present king of France*? How, given what you can call a general referential or denotational theory of meaning, where meanings are or are bound up with things stood for, can that happen? Certainly a very simple story won't work. Russell's theory of descriptions, to my mind, if famously not to Peter Strawson's liking, was and is a pretty good answer to the question.

Another striking piece of philosophy comes to mind at this point and might well have earlier. That is Searle's Chinese Room argument or thought experiment, the most enviable thing in the philosophy of mind in living memory. His summary of the argument is as follows.

A native English speaker who knows no Chinese is in a room with boxes of Chinese symbols (a database if you think of computers) together with instructions in English (a program) for manipulating the symbols. People outside send in Chinese symbols which, unknown to the English speaker, are questions in Chinese (the input). By following the instructions, syntactic rules governing the relations of signs to signs, he sends back Chinese symbols (the output) that in fact are correct answers to the questions. Everything he does has, in a sense, the right cause and effect. According to the theory or rather theories of relationism or computerism he should *understand* Chinese, but he doesn't.

Might the thought experiment also go in the direction of establishing that what he lacks is the consciousness that is *actual* consciousness? I'm not so clear about that now as back then, in that prolonged earlier conversation of mine, the much longer book of Actualism. Just a mistake on my part? Maybe not. It could be that Actualism is part of the strength or nerve of the Chinese Room argument.

Searle did and could just prove in a way independently that something *A* (for example, giving the right answers to the Chinese questions) is not what it has to be supposed to be in a theory, *B* (a case of understanding Chinese, being conscious in that way), without depending on another theory. Humble truths about *B*, common sense, what is unanalytic, not a theory, will do. By way of analogy, you can for a purpose – maybe showing something isn't liquid – depend on its not being *water* without knowing it's not H_2O.

We have to leave that troubling general matter unconsidered further. We also have to leave the general question of the extent to which various studies and researches, from linguistic representations to attitudes having to do with truth or want, and LOT, and facts in relationism or computerism, and so on, despite disagreements with them, *are* studies and researches in part consistent with and which can contribute to the theory of consciousness which we are on the way to completing. It is plain that they may in ways contribute to Actualism.

Also, with studies and researches in the science of consciousness, remember that fact is quite as essential as ordinary logic to progress. Partly because the two are not so easily separable as may be supposed.

You'll know, despite all my commitment to mutual respect, to coexistence, that it doesn't seem to me for a minute that we have to give up on the role of philosophy as against science with respect to consciousness. To revert to relationism or computerism, more in the practice of science than philosophy, there is that matter that we didn't linger over. This sentence printed on the page unread is a representation. So how far can representation itself go in explanation of the nature of cognitive and affective consciousness?

And something else. Suppose what we need to add to an account of cognitive and affective consciousness in terms of representation is something else, something in terms of *actual* consciousness, the *actuality* of consciousness. How much more will be added not in terms of just the figurative database and its summary, but in terms of the literal explanation, the theory or analysis of that actuality – added in terms of a certain subjective physicality?

ELEVEN

THINKING AND WANTING: BEING ACTUAL

O ur question now is what it is for representations to be actual – for the wide and various categories of thinkings and wantings to be actual. As you will anticipate from our philosophical encounter with subjective physical worlds, this actuality is a matter of characteristics, related to but not identical with either those of the objective physical world or the subjective physical worlds. This actuality adds up to the proposition that conscious representations are subjectively physical in their own way.

Representations - Their Physicality

Remembering that ordinary dictionaries define the physical as the non-mental, can there reasonably be hesitation about your now taking your conscious representations as physical in a subjective way? The answer depends, as before, on all the characteristics in the list, and so will be delayed until the end of it.

As you will also anticipate, the first part of the list has to do with physical characteristics – or the lack of them – and the second part with subjective characteristics.

(1) There can be no serious question about conscious representations having the particular characteristic of being physical that they are within the inventory of science. They are in there along with objective physical things and events generally and with the subjective physical worlds of perceptual consciousness. This is not only a matter of conscious representations in psychology and linguistics. The science of evolution itself has in it the emergence of language and its predecessors. So too of course is neuroscience inclusive of representations.

Do you say that it is a question whether the representations that are in science are representations conceived as those adequately initially clarified by us as actual consciousness? Well, one reply is that representations within science definitely are mainly if certainly not always primary ordinary ones, and we have no need of abandoning our having taken primary ordinary consciousness as actual consciousness.

Do you hark back, say, to Nagel's leading idea of something's being conscious, say a bat, as there being something it is like to be that thing? Do you ask if *that* is in science? It wasn't the case, despite intimations, that Nagel himself excluded it from science. Could it be that if 'what it's like to be something' were *not* in science, it wouldn't be as enlightening at all as to consciousness?

Do you happen to wonder, by the way, maybe wonder again, if our Actualism with its subjective representations is a dualism? A dreaded spiritualism? No.

Obviously it is not any dualism except in the unavoidable and trivial sense that any sane theory is – it makes a difference, some difference, between something, its subject, and something else, the rest of what there is. It makes *a* difference between consciousness and other physical stuff – objective physicality. So too do all arguable identifications and theories of consciousness as physical, find *some* difference of consciousness, including the thinking of such hardened materialists as Dennett. Given the necessity of recognizing the difference of consciouness, all arguable accounts of consciousness are at least trivially dualistic.

Our account, although you know already that it is within generic physicalism, the physical world that includes objective and subjective parts, gives a far greater difference to consciousness than any other such account – partly for additional and anticipated reasons to which we will come, about individuality.

(2) As of course is entailed by all this, conscious representations as we have identified them, representations whose nature we are investigating, are open to inquiry by the scientific method. Do you wonder in passing, before you go to a good book on scientific method, whether when you go to your optician to get your glasses changed and the capable woman asks for your beliefs about whether you can read the letters in the bottom row of the chart or are just guessing – do you wonder if you should exclude her carry-on, her reliance on your answer, from ordinary practical science?

Being rational, you don't. And, by the way, do you tend at any moment to raise about neuroscience the kind of superiority that was once indulged in about psychology?

(3) Conscious representations, we allow and have to allow, are unlike subjective physical worlds in perception, in that they are not somehow physical specifically in virtue of being given, had and so on *as* occupying space or in space. My thought that my mother's maiden name was Rae Laura Armstrong, even if all that stuff in the database is true of the thought, is not thereby in space. But my thought certainly isn't given and so on as *not* in space either. It certainly isn't given as abstract in any sense. But what to say, by the way, about my memory-image of Mother? Is that image given or had as spatial?

Do you say these uncertainties about conscious representations are a chink in my armour as an actualist about consciousness? Well, it is a necessary admission that things aren't simple about consciousness – and of course that as in the rest of philosophy we can't aspire to large proofs.

Is it possible, by the way, that more rather than less conviction can be had by a conclusion about consciousness if you have accepted that the conclusion, like others in philosophy, is not what it cannot aspire to be – proved? Whether or not that is so, what we need is realisms about each of philosophy and science, realisms about their natures.

But, to go back to where we were, the subject of space, there is no doubt about conscious representations and *time*. You can locate thoughts according to when you had them, according to clock and day. They're events, things that happen. And are there any things in time that aren't in space? To be in time is indeed to be a thing or event, and one of those has to be in space too, doesn't it? Discuss critically, as philosophy students at University College London used to be instructed in their final examination papers.

(4) Evidently particular conscious representations, as well as standing in conceptual connections with other such representations, connections of meaning, also stand in lawful connections with them, dependency relations – of which we have glanced at a decent understanding. It must be doubtful that anyone has ever made the audacious claim that particular thoughts and feelings do not cause one another.

(5) It is familiar that there are lawful connections between the category of conscious representations and other categories of things. The other category that should come to mind first is the category of subjective particular worlds, or more particularly stages of them. There are also the lawful connections fundamental

as any to our lives – between cognitive and affective representations. And of course between conscious representations and behaviour.

(6) Evidently conscious representations are not perceived. As evidently, they are in a way like items mentioned earlier in connection with objective physicality – things and events in what we called the microcosm. That is to say that conscious representations stand in lawful connection with perceived things, rooms and actions for a start.

(7) With representations, unlike objectively physical things and things in subjective physical worlds, there are not points of view. You can of course change your mind about representations in various ways, but representations are entirely remote from having different points of view with respect to a front door or a tree.

(8) Representations, implicit in what you have just heard, are not different from different points of view – of course in the sense in which things in the objective and the subjective physical worlds are different. Conscious representations do not have different perceived properties – sizes, parts, sides, aspects, relative locations and so on.

(9) Representations, in being actual, do not have primary and secondary properties. They don't have such primary properties as shape, size, motion or rest, solidity and number and they don't have such secondary properties as colour, sound, warmth and cold, and taste.

Representations – Their Subjectivity

(10) Conscious representations are of course not *separate* from facts of consciousness. They *are* some such facts, include them, are lawfully dependent on them.

(11) With conscious representations there is one particular representer. They are in a way and to an extent private rather than public. Conscious representations are in practice the possessions of only one particular perceiver.

(12) Conscious representations are such that one representer does have some privileged access to them – as remarked about subjective physical worlds, a greater confidence, certainly not infallibility.

(13) Conscious representations, cognitive ones, are reasonably taken to be less governed by the pursuit of factual truth and logic than judgements with objective physical things are or are presumed to be, partly because of not being public. Maybe we need an exception with respect to judgements on objective physical things as judged in politics, first in the tradition of conservatism.

(14) If conscious representations as subjective raise problems and indeed are challenges to scientific method, they are not beyond it. They are not beyond the method sometimes said to include clarification or characterization, theory or hypothesis, prediction and testing.

(15) Like your subjective physical world, your representations are a great component of the particular fact of subjectivity that is your individuality, mentioned a few times already but of which there is more to be considered at the best time – in the next, twelfth and last phase of all this inquiry, when we look at everything that's been put on the table between us.

But to say a few words now, this individuality will be no spooky self or the like, but a unity over time owed to and indeed united by dependencies and interdependencies of lawfulness and meaning. It is a unity containing cognitive and affective consciouness including memory and anticipation and of course involving more of the mental than consciousness.

(16) Reverting now to that question delayed at the start until we got through this list, the above physical and subjective properties of conscious representations, in contrast to objective physical properties, are *not* good cause for hesitancy about consciousness consisting in them. There *are* those differences from objective physicality.

One thing to be said about all this, to go back again to the style of Berkeley's aphorism *To be is to be perceived*, is that our aphorism for the cognitive and affective part of a wholly different theory is again something not so snappy. *To be cognitively or affectively conscious is for a kind of thing, representations, in a way to be – neither the same things nor in exactly the same way as with perceptual consciousness.*

One larger matter to be contemplated now in connection with our physicality list for cognitive and affective consciousness has to do with what you heard of earlier in passing, Jerry Fodor's despair about understanding what he speaks of as representation, aboutness, the semantic or, in a traditional way, as intentionality. Here is his statement of despair.

I suppose that sooner or later the physicists will complete the catalogue they've been compiling of the ultimate and irreducible properties of things. When they do, the likes of *spin*, *charm*, and *charge* will perhaps appear upon their list. But *aboutness* surely won't; intentionality simply doesn't go that deep. It's hard to see, in the face of this consideration, how one can be a Realist about intentionality without also being, to some extent or other, a Reductionist. If the semantic and the intentional are real properties of things, it must be in virtue of their identity with (or maybe their supervenience on?) properties that are themselves neither intentional nor semantic. If aboutness is real, it must be really something else.

Is the point to be taken as being that aboutness or representation in general, that widest category, the wholly general category, is the mystifying problem? Surely not.

And the problem or mystery in question is not shared with, I'm pretty sure, the aboutness or representation in itself that is only a printed sentence on a page – a printed sentence no one is reading, a printed sentence of which no one is aware. That the thing remains a representation in a clear sense is beyond doubt, of course. The conventions or like facts that connect it to something evidently do not depend on someone reading it. Whatever the interest and questions with any such representation, it is as much a representation in this way as, say, an unseen photo of you.

Fodor, in speaking of aboutness, must be speaking of aboutness in another sense. He *must* be taken as speaking of, exactly of – *conscious aboutness, conscious representation.* Certainly, you can refer to a conscious representation by speaking just of a representation, an aboutness – as indeed we often have, along with everybody else.

So – what Fodor takes to be needed is a theory or analysis of *consciousness* in representing, in thinking and wanting. It is reasonable enough for sharp Susan Schneider at the University of Connecticut to note ungentlemanly the absence of such a theory or analysis in his work – note what she calls the absence of an elephant in the room. What is needed, on an ordinary assumption, is an account of consciousness in thinking and wanting, consciousness with representations, that goes together with an account of consciousness generally.

If there is still some more to be said about it, we have such a theory – are well on the way to its summation. We have it without embracing what Fodor presumably has in mind, a reductionism – which often enough is rightly taken as *not* being an account of what is said to be reduced. Not giving the nature of something but rather the attempt to put something else in its place. Changing the subject to a different related one that is more manageable in a line of life, a kind of inquiry, more manageable than ordinary consciousness. There is much of this, it needs to be reported without elaboration or indeed explanation, in cognitive science.

But my main proposition here is something else, something simple. It is that *we* don't explain conscious representation by reducing it to something else, maybe abandoning the real subject. We actualists explain conscious representation by *adding* something, a large thing, to representation – to representation exemplified by a printed sentence on a page and also to just a counterpart of it in cognitive or affective consciousness. Our account isn't reductive, but, so to speak, the opposite – it is a complete account, necessarily enlarging or ampliative account, obviously necessarily so. Of course it is realist in an ordinary sense of the word.

To speak differently, the full story for me and maybe for you, the true story of conscious representations, the stuff of cognitive and affective consciousness, is not a matter of only a two-term relation, however complex. It is also a matter of *the actuality of the representations*, their being *subjectively physical*. That additional fact is best or anyway well described in terms of the fact of the representations as being within the great fact of individuality with respect to anything that enjoys cognitive and affective consciousness as well as perceptual consciousness. Starts with bees, spiders, locusts and other arthropods, according to Burge.

So – with conscious representation it is my proposal to you that we have got something here worth having, a solution to Fodor's despair.

We cannot for a moment conclude that the whole subject of representations and conscious representations has been laid bare, the story anything like fully told. The philosophy and science on it is indeed a labyrinth of terms, ideas, theories, doctrines and attitudes. This higher Disneyland, to think of a previous and longer tour of it, the one called *Actual Consciousness*, is such that it is possible for the tour guide himself to get lost on returning to it.

Thank God for standing-for, the simplicity of the dyadic relation, something's being connected by semantic and syntactic conventions to something else. Clear enough. Remember naming children. But there is lots of complication. How is linguistic representation related to lingualism? and both to representational naturalism?

Thank God too for another clear enough fact, our large new one which was and is *Conscious Representation = Representation + Actuality*. It's not that *Conscious Representation = Conscious Representation Reduced to Something Else* or *Conscious Representation with Something Left Out*.

Is there an annoying question of whether cognitive and affective consciousness, consciousness with representations, asks for further explanation having to do with something else that is only vague?

We have the fact that representations *carry the mind* to what is represented. That is what it is for them to represent. Can it be, as was wondered earlier, that we need with cognitive and affective consciousness to look into the possible need for some further carrying? Some additional role here, to be quick, of subjective physical worlds? You are excused my further struggle here. Maybe you can say something about it yourself, guide your own tour.

And another, maybe smaller question. Are we to take it that the attitudes having to do with truth and what is somehow good are to be taken as always *parts* of what is represented in conscious representation? Or are the attitudes, which must be in the story of conscious representation somehow, to be treated differently, maybe quite differently? Spend thinking time on that yourself.

And still something else, larger, worth lingering over a bit, here or somewhere else. Do you now think more assertively what was contemplated earlier, that we've made a suspect or dubious *leap* from actual consciousness, consciousness as understood in that database, implicitly consciousness in its three sides, to representations and also worlds as now understood, representations and worlds as *subjectively physical*? That it is not a step of argument, that there is no train of argument to support the proposition of subjective physical representations and worlds?

A reply exists. There *is* the fact that those figurative perceptions in the database are already both ontic and epistemic. They are about the existence of things and also about knowledge with respect to them. The defined existence of subjective physical representations and worlds flows from that existence of something gestured at. The dependence of my world on what is in my head as well as the external objective physical world is one continuity from the data having to do with existence and certainty.

But that is not all that contributed at least naturally to the general idea of the three sides of consciousness as subjectively physical. Reconsider the previous theories of consciousness at which we glanced, from traditional dualism, that anti-physicalism and abstract functionalism, on through, say, non-naturalism, physical intentionality and supervenience, such particular physicalisms as those of Searle and Dennett.

It is hardly too much to say that this preoccupation with the physical, in affirmation and particularizing and denial, say denial with Chalmers and Hannay, is evidence that a solution to the consciousness problem was to be found in consideration of the physical. In addition to the subject of consciousness, what else was there?

That is still not all. Remember the criteria. Remember not only the first two, about *the actual*, but also the criterion of the reality of consciousness, the criterion of naturalness, and the criterion of a side of consciousness having to do with perception rather than thought or feeling. Also the criterion of connections to brain and behaviour.

You've heard from me a few times my conviction that philosophy does not consist in proofs of large things. How could it, by the way, since the traditional large proofs, say the large proofs with respect to the existence of God, are all of them arguments that are in fact disputed and denied? Of course it has not been insisted or suggested that subjective physicality was forced on us by deductive or inductive logic.

So it is not being proposed that we have been, so to speak, J. M. Synge's Philosophical Playboy of the Western World, but have stepped along carefully enough. Remember too what is relevant, those declarations from other philosophers about the need to get into higher gear, attempt philosophical revolution and so on.

And a further piece of assertion here, maybe supported by the reality of inquiry and argument. Yes, we do indeed say that our premise was the database and our conclusion was the subjective physicality of representations and worlds. But, you may agree, the conclusion stands up itself.

There is persuasiveness in the account of the three sides of consciousness as subjectively physical. Some of it would be there if it were taken alone, not got from the database. The account does indeed fit nicely with the preoccupation with the objectively physical, *both* assertion and denial of it, in the history of reflection on consciousness, and also fits with our criteria.

What about the idea, then, maybe not a shocker, that our conclusion confers a recommendation on our premise? That we can argue backwards as well as forwards. That we can reason contrapositively not only from a case of *if p then q*, from the persuasiveness of the database to that of the theory – but also from *if not q then not p*, from the independent persuasiveness of the theory to that of the database. Discuss critically.

TWELVE

A SUMMARY TABLE OF PHYSICALITIES

L ook back. We contemplated, at the start, what was then less obvious than it is now: that disagreement about the nature of what it is to be conscious in the primary ordinary or core sense has been and is at least significantly the result of people talking about different things. It transpired there was good support for this.

None of the five leading ideas of consciousness gave an adequate initial clarification of the subject. Various theories of consciousness, although we did not pause to consider the matter, gave evidence of different initial proccupations or orientations. Say the instance of consciousness taken so extraordinarily as *all* of the mental, including *all* the causally relevant neural what-not.

We did arrive at our clarification of ordinary consciousness by way of a kind of tacit unanimity in the usages of the proponents of the five leading ideas and also other people. Our database gave a more than inchoate summary of consciousness as *something's being actual* – a figurative summary suggesting both ontic or existential and also epistemic facts.

Then, at least prompted also by the various concerns with physicality in the raft of existing theories of consciousness – dualism

and abstract functionalism and then a lot more – we eschewed
a certain high generality – thereby, alas, maybe embarrassingly,
raising a unopened question about what the true generalness of
philosophy can comprise. Anyway, we assembled characteristics
of the objective physical world.

Do you hope with me that particularity can serve a philosophically proper generalness? The hope was too superior and too
large in past Oxford for a while. As you've heard, J. L. Austin the
dictionary-philosopher vs the not so fastidious but philosophically
more robust A. J. Ayer.

From the objective physical world, we went on to the question
of *what* is actual with consciousness in perception, and the answer
of subjective physical worlds, say a stage of one, a room. Then on
to the following question of what its actuality consists in. There
was the answer of its having characteristics that are counterparts,
in ways different, of those of the objective physical world.

Next, the analysis or theory of consciousness as a whole was
taken forward by the consideration of cognitive and affective
consciousness. What is actual here are representations, maybe
including attitudes to what in a narrower sense is represented, attitudes different in the two cases, one having to do with truth and
the other with value, more basically want. Affirming and valuing
representations. The representations being actual was their being
subjectively physical, similarly but also differently so from from
the case of perceptual consciousness.

Of that whole theory of Actualism there is the full summary
that is the following table – anticipated back at the very beginning
– a table of categories.

By way of a briefer reminder, your being conscious in perception is a state of affairs that consists in a subjective world external
to you, dependent on both the external objective physical world

and on you. Your being conscious in perception, again, is *not* a state of affairs named as content or the like of the hitherto dominant theories of perceptual consciousness, *not* a state of affairs that consists in your having conscious representations – of the objectively physical external world. Give up on all that.

But your being cognitively or affectively conscious *is* an existence of representations, that state of affairs which also includes dependencies. Our conception of conscious representations is not subject to Fodor's despair about aboutness. Conscious aboutness *is* real and it is not something else.

That our Actualism is both an externalism and an internalism, unique in the extents to which it is both, has been wholly a response to the question that is the nature of ordinary consciousness. That it is *a* physicalism about consciousness, a unique physicalism, separate indeed from objective, devout scientific or standard physicalism, is one of its principal uniquenesses – the others being the database from which it begins, and the combination of both externalism and internalism about consciousness, and the role of subjective physical worlds with perceptual consciousness.

The physicalism of Actualism, evidently, is a matter of the argued genus that is physicality in general dividing into species that are objective physicality and subjective physicality, and the subspecies of subjective physicality that are subjective physical worlds and subjective representations.

Actualism has had no source at all in anything grander. It does not have the distinction of being a form of Bertrand Russell's neutral monism, as has been contemplated. To hazard a summary of that, it is the proposition that what *really* exists is a simple kind of primal stuff, primitive elements, neutral between being physical and being mental. Still, see Ingmar Persson's different reflections.

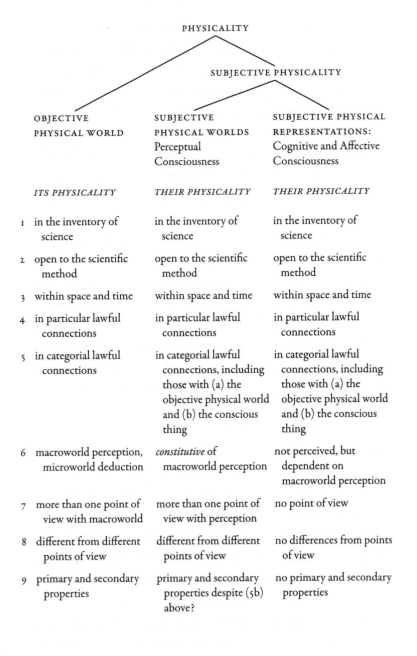

PHYSICALITY

SUBJECTIVE PHYSICALITY

OBJECTIVE PHYSICAL WORLD	SUBJECTIVE PHYSICAL WORLDS Perceptual Consciousness	SUBJECTIVE PHYSICAL REPRESENTATIONS: Cognitive and Affective Consciousness
ITS PHYSICALITY	*THEIR PHYSICALITY*	*THEIR PHYSICALITY*
1 in the inventory of science	in the inventory of science	in the inventory of science
2 open to the scientific method	open to the scientific method	open to the scientific method
3 within space and time	within space and time	within space and time
4 in particular lawful connections	in particular lawful connections	in particular lawful connections
5 in categorial lawful connections	in categorial lawful connections, including those with (a) the objective physical world and (b) the conscious thing	in categorial lawful connections, including those with (a) the objective physical world and (b) the conscious thing
6 macroworld perception, microworld deduction	*constitutive* of macroworld perception	not perceived, but dependent on macroworld perception
7 more than one point of view with macroworld	more than one point of view with perception	no point of view
8 different from different points of view	different from different points of view	no differences from points of view
9 primary and secondary properties	primary and secondary properties despite (5b) above?	no primary and secondary properties

ITS OBJECTIVITY	THEIR SUBJECTIVITY	THEIR SUBJECTIVITY
10 separate from consciousness	not separate from consciousness	not separate from consciousness
11 public	private	private
12 common access	some privileged access	some privileged access
13 truth and logic, more subject to?	truth and logic, less subject to?	truth and logic, less subject to?
14 open to the scientific method	open to the scientific method despite doubt	open to the scientific method, despite doubt
15 includes no self or unity or other such inner fact of subjectivity inconsistent with the above properties of the objective physical world	each subjective physical world is an element in an individuality that is a unique and large unity of lawful and conceptual dependencies including much else	each representation is an element in an individuality that is a unique and large unity of lawful and conceptual dependencies including much else
16 hesitation about whether objective physicality includes consciousness	no significant hesitation about taking the above subjective physicality as being that of actual perceptual consciousness	no significant hesitation about taking this subjective physicality as being the nature of actual cognitive and affective consciousness

Also, Actualism has not come at all, of course, from that great confrontation in the history of philosophy already mentioned between the materialists or physicalists and the so-called idealists, between materialist French and so on and such elevated and elevating Germans and English as the metaphysicians Hegel and Bradley.

But to say a word of this coincidence with that great historical contradiction, you may yourself contemplate the courageous idea that the existence of the great confrontation is a piece of distant and past evidence for the need of a fundamental compromise about the nature of consciousness. Was the confrontation itself, in general terms about consciousness and the material, the existence of both sides of it, a small collateral support for Actualism? Also, did the confrontation have an origin in as yet unspoken and unsung Actualism within the philosophy of mind? Anyway an intimation of it? You can put that question in a pigeonhole next to that of the larger question of the real worth of a kind of consensus in contemporary philosophy and science.

Actualism has had no source either in, say, residual disagreement in our own century between objective, scientific or standard physicalism and its adversaries, a disagreement so nicely contemplated by Crane and Mellor under the brave title 'There is No Question of Physicalism'.

Maybe, at this culminating moment of the comparative table summarizing nearly all our progress, you revert to objections we have considered in the course of that progress – or still more from the thinking of the graduate student made very good Paul Noordhof? Do you revert to the zombie objection, maybe engage in mere science fiction? Do you say that either a living thing or a computer could have the two right-hand columns of the table true of it and not be at all conscious in our primary ordinary sense?

That can be denied pretty confidently, for more than the reason given earlier, the fact of the possibility and occurrence of illusions, not only such a personal illusion as that you've got diabetes but widely shared illusions. Illusions, you might say, that are a culture or anyway pervasive in a culture.

My greater grounds of denial now are of course the performances of Actualism as against other theories of consciousness in satisfying those criteria we put together for a successful theory of consciousness. If Actualism is philosophical, an exercise in concentration on the logic of intelligence, and harder than the science that admits of proofs, does it not perform pretty decently in terms of the list of criteria? Look again.

Pass by quickly the first *two* of those conditions of adequacy – answers to what is actual and to what the actuality consists in – and then consider the conditions that might be thought more important by someone in that they do not flow directly from our own initial clarification of consciousness.

There is Actualism's satisfying of the *third* criterion, that of reality, most importantly its perfect acceptance of the fact of the causation by consciousness of physical actions and the rest. There is no difficulty, although we did not pause to consider the matter, of taking the subjectively physical to be causal with respect to the objectively physical, or the other way on.

Are you still tempted to linger over the question of the extent of the satisfying of the *fourth* condition, that an acceptable theory must make consciousness *different*? Satisfying this criterion that has preserved to this day the vestigial existence of dualism in, say, the neuroscience of the brave Chalmers and also preserved the innocent persistence of abstract functionalism in both the philosophy of mind and cognitive science?

Are you tempted to cavil with the proposition that subjective physicalism of the several kinds is quite enough to give us the fundamental difference of consciousness? Are you insufficiently moved by the propositions that are in no other theory of consciousness – the propositions of subjective physical worlds, of two species of physicality, objective and subjective, in the genus that is the physical world?

Along with subjective physical worlds, as a result also of what is said of cognitive and affective consciousness, we have both an externalism and an internalism with respect to consciousness. We have what was surely necessary, a very different account of conscious representation.

As you have heard before now, we certainly have in sum *more* clarified and unobjectionable difference, more content in our propositions of difference, than is had by dualism or abstract functionalism. We have a lot more difference than in flat objective physicalisms, whatever the efforts of proponents. It's surely true, isn't it, that Actualism does better in this way than the strong and valorous work of Chalmers, Dennett, Searle and others? And lays Chalmers's hard problem of consciousness to rest? So I trust, anyway hope happily.

There is something else that you may agree is of yet greater importance, a firmer ground of judgement in favour of Actualism with respect to registering the difference of consciousness. This is Actualism's satisfying of the related criterion – the *fifth* – having to do with subjectivity. Come on to this, of which you heard an anticipation earlier.

It has to be allowed and maintained that the demand for an understanding of talk and impulses having to do with subjectivity has had obscurity about it. More particularly, what has led to the contemplation of the idea of a metaphysical self, a kind of phantom boat of personhood sailing on in or over the waters of your experience, is definitely and merely valiantly obscure. Are the grounds of persisting mistakes always obscure?

What has to be said quickly and bravely at this point is that Actualism's satisfying of the criterion of subjectivity, much owed to others, notably the personal-identity people, is the best satisfying of the criteria known to me. Certainly in the best kind. Recall the theory's rich conception of the unity of a conscious thing, the individuality of a conscious thing. It is a unity owed not to a mystery homunculus or an internal flashlight, or maybe a soul or some other other inner thing, maybe something from Freud. Rather it is a unity owed to the oneness of a great thing over time, over a life, not far off from being a life itself. Something of course under-described as a *thing*, better called a unity united by lawful and other dependencies, including something of physical functionalism and what takes work to think about and maybe make clear, the seeming dependency of parts on the whole.

But, you may cavil, this is the unity of what is also rightly spoken of as personal identity not only in the work of the contemporary leader of the subject, successor to Locke, Derek Parfit of Oxford and New York. Is this an objection? Surely not. It is satisfactory to be able to make use of a strong line of thinking from another place. Locke and Parfit are such as to advance a cause.

There is a still larger reply. Your individuality, your identity, in Actualism, includes what has certainly not been part of good thinking at all on personal identity, *a subjective physical world*. There is, literally, an absolutely unique and ongoing real place of your life.

It is too late in this conversation for us to think and maybe feel more on the matter. It can be said, though, that we have here a singular satisfying of the criterion of consciousness spoken of in terms of subjectivity. An ongoing personal place as part of and indeed fundamental to the conception of a person. *A life-world.* We are a long way beyond James's *stream.* Beyond an image that relatively speaking is weak and does not rise to its subject.

It is not too late in this conversation to think and say something else, already implied in various stages and moments of it. It is a denial of contentions noted in several stages and to be a little elaborated below. Actualism gives us the conclusion that there simply is no *unique* mystery of consciousness. That is close to another true proposition, that Actualism gives us the conclusion that consciousness is as much a subject for science as anything else.

Of course there are remaining problems in the theory, fairly large ones. Yes again, Actualism is as much a workplace as a theory. That is also to be seen as the recommendation of which you have heard, that it is a fertile theory.

There is also the *sixth* criterion – the three sides of consciousness – of which no more needs to be said.

The *seventh* criterion, naturalism, was understood by us ordinarily in terms of acceptance of things open to the scientific method. Evidently Actualism *is* a naturalism. There is of course no problem of what used to be called the ghost in the machine, the ghost written out of most philosophy in *The Concept of Mind* by Gilbert Ryle, something traditionally spiritual, but not replaced. In Actualism no ghost of a ghost either, as in abstract functionalism and much related cognitive science. Actualism declares to us no inexplicable thing.

Yes, it leaves all of consciousness indubitably a subject for science, a subject which, despite awful and wonderful complexity, is known not to have in it any barrier to knowledge different in kind from everything else. Actualism may be able to liberate a scientist or two from a hesitancy about consciousness research.

But over this important matter of Actualism's indubitably opening all of consciousness to science, we can and should take more time. Many more related reminders come to mind here to reassure and encourage the scientists among us. Here are a baker's dozen or so.

As several of the above propositions entail, it would be entirely mistaken, indeed benighted, to suppose what used to be and still is supposed, that science deals with and can deal only with those *neural correlates* of consciouness, not consciousness itself. That is a fallacy that wholly wrongly diminishes science. One other fallacy, already in the past, is that impertinent notion that there is a self that owns a brain.

Is the idea that your being perceptually conscious *is* a real world out there, absolutely not a world in the head – is this different idea strange enough to call for serious laboratorial doubt, maybe more than that, maybe a temptation or even an inclination to set this theory in its extraordinariness aside from science in its extraordinariness?

If so, you are in your conventionality forgetting other large extraordinariness. That physics-with-metaphysics not only on television of 'the universe', imagining its beginning in space and time. The subjects of space and time themselves. Schrödinger's Cat and the like. Science is not short of what is too kindly celebrated as the extraordinary. It is not just a matter of the wonderful stuff offered in interpretation of the mathematics of quantum theory.

In some connection with strangeness, by the way, there is no easy distinction between science and philosophy in the matter of respect for consensus, for that kind of democracy about truth. Philosophy is not alone in trying to upset applecarts. Remember the great scientific revolutions. They went against and destroyed consensus. Day-to-day science seeks to unsettle itself, and does.

Yes, to affirm again, actual consciousness is wholly within what science admits to what it takes to exist, its inventory of reality, physicality generally – despite the width of science's primary concern with objective physicality. Further, the reality of actual consciousness also does not deprive it of the great fact of consciousness, on which the mistake of dualism tries to depend but cannot – the great fact that we have consciousness as not only real but different. While being real, it is subjective.

The facts of its physicality and of its subjectivity, as you have heard, can be made wholly explicit. They are not and cannot be made simpler than they are. It is proposed to you again that Actualism follows Newton in letting reality speak for itself.

To go on with the baker's dozen of thoughts about Actualism and science, being actually conscious is to be understood in terms of naturalism, further, in that it is to be understood as being a state of affairs wholly open in principle to understanding by way of the scientific method. It is to be added, of course, that it is a state of affairs also to be understood, also to be contributed to, by a method that is true not only to a critical empiricism but also, as you remember, to concentration on an ordinary logic that is clarity, consistency and validity, completeness, generalness.

It is a good idea for science to remember a passing remark of a philosopher more esteemed by me than all or almost all of his contemporaries, Peter Strawson. The remark, about philosophy, was 'Science is not only the offspring of common sense; it remains its dependant.'

Are you a philosopher, however, inclined by my attitude to science to bring up the mistake of scientism? At least excessive confidence in the power of science, sometimes boyish or girlish dismissal of anything else? Yes, there is that silly mistake. There is also the silly mistake of philosophism. One of its saints is Wittgenstein. He should be better known than he is for what is to me the egregious effrontery, so true to his Viennese past, that 'no supposition seems more natural than that there is no process in the brain correlated with associating or thinking.'

Actual consciousness, as needs to be declared one last time, is obviously a subject that is open to and can be clarified by science. Do you say that so too can another subject sometimes called consciousness? That is what for Actualism is both conscious and unconscious mentality taken together, mentioned and considered already.

But our actual consciousness arguably is the subject uniquely necessary to *all* such inquiry, certainly necessary to the very identification of unconscious mentality. It is what distinguishes, for a start, the unconscious mental from musculature in the explanation of behaviour.

Do you, since your guide is a philosopher, and despite some previous remarks, still wonder about what place the science of the mind and in particular the science of consciousness is given in his inquiry? Well, it has in it the inclination, resolution and indeed certainty on the part of your guide that a good theory of consciousness must give a prime place to the science of the mind and consciousness. If the philosophy does not actually engage in the science, the philosophy cannot assign to itself only an ancillary role. A good philosophy of consciousness can no more make the science of it into a handmaiden of itself than decent philosophy can be what Locke supposed, merely a handmaiden of science.

After that baker's dozen of reminders in connection with the criterion of naturalism and science, there is also the eighth and last criterion having to do with the *relations* of consciousness, in fact bound up with the seventh – and not the first thing bound up with another in an attempt to make sense of whatever is a real challenge. The eighth criterion, notably, is spoken of as the relation of consciousness to the brain, also known traditionally as the mind–body problem.

You will not need reassuring that for Actualism there is no 'hard problem' of the brain–consciousness connection. It is done for. There is no foundation at all for the idea. The only connection in question is that foundation and staple of science, lawful connection, certainly clearly explicable.

It takes bravery but, to lovely Chomsky's stunning declaration that there is no sense or worthwhile content or coherence in consideration of the mind–body problem, there is now the possibility of a further reply. It is the reply that is the sum of all that you have heard of the relations with respect to perceptual consciousness and the other two sides of consciousness. There's sense there in those particulars.

It evidently has a basis in science, whatever other such basis it may lack, and it has the great additional basis of the rest of our knowledge. The worth and force of that judgement against Chomsky's scepticism, at this late minute, is something more for you in private reflection. Go to it. Maybe my private reflection too. Maybe public reflection some other time.

There remains a question to which an answer was promised back at the very beginning, that of the right subject with respect to the philosophy and science of consciousness.

Was ordinary consciousness, consciousness in the primary ordinary sense, the core sense, the right consciousness to consider? Was actual consciousness, which *is* that ordinary consciousness, therefore the right subject? Should we instead have joined a lot of science and thought about consciousness where it has in it, undistinguished, both what is for us actual consciousness, and, in the same sense of 'conscious', unconscious mentality?

However misleading a title just including 'consciousness' would have been for that wider concern, it would have been *as right* a subject as concern with actual consciousness. There is no serious sense in which there is *the* right subject here. But, as you have heard, there is a uniquely necessary subject – ours. For a start, as you heard a minute ago, the very definition of the mental, all of the mental in any sense, depends on the idea of ordinary consciousness.

To which I am tempted to add while it occurs to me, or add again, in connection with Chomsky and physicality and physics and the mind–body problem, that there must be more than a question as to the existence of *the right conception* of the physical, the one and only. But I leave that to you and him.

Another thought in farewell. Since you have often heard from me the name *actual consciousness*, it may have crossed your mind, as it did Hannay's, that the consciousness laid out in our theory was so named not just on account of a database on it but also in order to imply that this consciousness is the real thing, what exists, the genuine article, what we all have a hold on, nothing else – that the theory gives us the nature of the reality of our consciousness, isn't any of the false consciousnesses laid out in other theories.

That wasn't intended. It's a little vague to me in seeming to go beyond the matter of our having really been concerned with consciousness in our primary ordinary sense. But maybe it's got truth in it.

And one more thought. Do some of the five leading ideas we began with, and some of the previous theories or analyses of consciousness, come to a fruition or a further fruition in Actualism? An explicitness? Certainly there are parallel concerns in leading ideas, other theories, and Actualism.

Maybe fruition with respect to the leading ideas of intentionality and what it's like to be something? Content for what that latter idea comes to? Much more content for traditional subjectivity? And for the theories of dualism and conceivably abstract functionalism, and for physicalism? For naive realism certainly, and for representationisms and supervenience theories and the previous general but limited externalisms? For common-sense belief and indeed truism about perception as of course involving both us and reality? The psychology of perception?

Maybe those questions and all this reflection on philosophy and science is too spirited for you? Too confident? A philosopher up on his hind legs? Without purporting to join or to be equal to or to be approximate to them, I refer you to philosophers and scientists past and present. Not that hopeful and slightly absurd scientist who announced a few years ago that philosophy is dead.

Rather Newton and Chomsky. The first indeed said, let nature speak for itself. The second overturned an orthodoxy in linguistics and related science, and went on to do what should have overturned orthodoxies about international relations and his own country's role in them. What the rest of us can do is try to emulate them – which, as you will rightly note, does not require entire agreement.

The very last thought. Is Actualism a fertile theory in terms of more than ongoing philosophy of mind, neuroscience, psychology and cognitive science? Fertile outside these neighbourhoods? Is there an instance additional to one or two already noted?

Well, yes, Actualism does something more to rid us further of a problem over centuries of either the logical compatibility or the logical incompability of the concept of determinism and the concept of freedom, Hume on one side, Kant on the other, a problem first cracked, in my opinion, in a longer and then a shorter book.

There is no such logical problem since we do have *both* a concept or idea of voluntariness and a concept or idea of origination – whatever else is to be said of and against the second one. (i) Freedom as sensible voluntariness, at bottom doing what you want, and (ii) freedom as the primitive idea of an uncaused but somehow controlled origination of choices and decisions. The right response to the compatibilist and incompatibilist traditions, then, is that we have *both* a compatible and an incompatible idea.

Actualism helps in a way by including a newly articulated and full account of voluntariness in terms of individuality or personal identity – that lawful corpus. A freedom, I cannot resist saying again, that is the reality of free choice as the lawful issue from a rich unity, not a merely mysterious willing only uncertainly connected with a person's past. Rather the real freedom that is the voluntariness that is a man's or a woman's existence issuing in thought and action.

Two more remarks on consciousness and freedom are possible. The first has to do with *standing*. As has been well seen by such friends of origination as Robert Kane of Texas, also the leader of the whole subject of determinism and freedom, our human desire for free will as against voluntariness, if we still have it, is at bottom a desire for human standing.

You get a lot of real standing, no guff, by having a subjective physical world dependent on you as well as on the objective physical world. You can think and reflect on and feel that. It is important in more than the present context, say with philosophies of life. But, to stick to the present context, can we persuade American Baptists and Pentecostals, and even members of the Conservative party in English politics, so keen on what they and others deserve, to give up the subject of free will and join the century we are in?

I'm made a little uneasy by the fact that they won't also be led into the light of rationality by a philosopher of whom you've heard my admiration – none other than Searle. Well we can't all be perfect all the time.

A last remark on consciousness and freedom. In Tolstoy's *War and Peace*, as many remember, Natasha at prayer says to herself that even if she cannot understand, still she cannot doubt. Forget the religion. But think that if you can't understand something, you can't literally and really believe it. Actualism with respect to freedom and such attached things as the standing of responsibility gives us what we *can* believe – not the mere mystery of origination but a real freedom bound up with real subjectivity, with a unity and individuality that is the reality of a person.

That's it. To revert to our main subject, don't go back to sleep with the five leading ideas about consciousness or all those other theories of it or more conventional philosophy of mind – or unmesmerizing stuff from Wittgenstein – or go half asleep with cognitive science. And don't fall back into philosophical pessimism about consciousness.

If you want a lot more awakening towards what may be truth or a further approximation to it, get a thing that follows exactly the same sequence as this conversation now ended, its 2014 predecessor. A book five bloody times as long though.

You'll find that the conversation now ended is not a recantation in general of the earlier one. But, as remarked way back there at the beginning, it does have further thoughts and different thoughts in it, quite a few, and at least new hopes.

GLOSSARY

aboutness The property of a representation, say of a word or image or a related conscious thing, in virtue of which it represents or is about or means or stands for something else. A property sometimes thought to be mysterious. *See also* representation, intentionality.

abstract functionalism The idea that the nature of a conscious event or state is somehow a functional role, that is, a relation to causes and effects or other other things, and that the event or state, which may be correlated with a neural or other physical event or state, is not itself physical, but abstract. *See also* physical functionalism, multiple realizability.

access consciousness Contrasted by Block with phenomenal or ordinary consciousness. Open to being critically understood as consisting in what has commonly been known as dispositional belief and dispositional attitudes generally. *See also* dispositional belief.

actual consciousness as initially clarified In the theory of this book and in the related book *Actual Consciousness*, of which this one is a summary and more, actual consciousness is consciousness in our primary ordinary or core sense, identified in a general way as something's being actual through a database as to our use of the word 'consciousness'. *See also* database, actual consciousness. *See also* actual consciousness as analysed, its nature.

actual consciousness as analysed, its nature, what can be maintained to be the defensible theory or analysis of it Actual consciousness clarified as something's being actual is, on analysis, its being subjectively physical, differently so in perceptual consciousness, cognitive consciousness and affective consciousness. *Go to* the Summary Table of Physicalities, Chapter Twelve.

actual consciousness database *See* database, actual consciousness.

actual representations being such in theory of cognitive and affective consciousness. Just their being in their own way subjectively physical.

actual, something being Either (1) something's being adequately initially identified or clarified by the general property of being actual, derived from a database, or (2) something's being analysed as having a subjectively physical nature, different in the case of perceptual consciousness as against cognitive and affective consciousness.

actual stages or worlds being such in theory of *perceptual* **consciousness** Stages and worlds being in a unique way subjectively physical.

actual, what is, in *cognitive and affective* **consciousness** Representations, subjectively physical, comprising attiutdes related either to truth or to goodness.

Actualism (1) The adequate initial clarification of ordinary consciousness, consciousness in the primary ordinary sense, the core sense, as actual consciousness. Or (2) the theory or analysis of this consciousness in terms of subjective physicalities, different in the cases of consciousness in perception, cognitive consciousness and affective consciousness. Or (3) both.

actuality The property of something's being actual, that is, having a general property characterized in a database of our related ideas about ordinary consciousness.

actuality of conscious representations Their being actual is their being subjectively physical, differently so from the being actual of subective physical worlds.

actuality of subjective physical worlds Their being actual is their being subjectively physical, differently so from the being actual of representations.

adequate initial clarification of subject of consciousness An identification of a subject adequate to ensure that discussion, inquiry, research or dispute concerns a single question, maybe a matter of real rather than only seeming dispute. Necessary for a satisfactory theory or analysis of consciousness.

affective consciousness Kinds of wanting – as against the kinds of thinking that are cognitive consciousness. Thus representations, including sentences, having to do with desire or goodness. *Cf.* perceptual consciousness, an existence of subjective physical worlds. *Go to* the Summary Table of Physicalities, Chapter Twelve.

anomalous monism Davidson's theory of mind or consciousness to the effect that there is one thing in question but not as a matter of law. Incomprehensible to those who take lawful connection or denial of it to be a matter of two things.

aspectual theories Theories of consciousness, including panpsychism and neutral monism, that assign two different aspects to a conscious thing, state or event – an inner and outer one, or a conscious and an unconscious one, or two organizations of a single neutral stuff.

attending, attention In the special sense used in psychology and elsewhere, attending is thinking or feeling about something particular within perception, within the subjective physical world. Hence special cases of cognitive and affective consciousness.

attitudes The stuff of cognitive and affective consciousness, as against perceptual consciousness. This stuff being representations related to truth or goodness – truth in the case of cognitive consciousness, goodness in the case of affective consciousness.

awareness Often taken as consciousness. Sometimes offered, surely circularly, in definitions of consciousness.

behaviourism As generally or anyway often understood, the idea that consciousness is to be understood in terms of behaviour. According to behaviourism, terms or concepts for conscious states can be and should be replaced by or reduced to terms or concepts for behaviour.

categorial lawful connections Lawful connections between categories of things, for example, subjective physical worlds, and the representations of them in cognitive and affective consciousness, rather than between individual things as against categories.

causal circumstance *See* circumstance, causal.

causal connection The main kind of lawful connection, in which one of the connected things precedes the other in time.

characteristics of physicality Some are the same, some different, in each of (i) objective physicality, (ii) subjective physicality of perceptual consciousness, (iii) subjective physicality of cognitive and affective consciousness.

circularity The uselessness or failing in giving, of a term x, a definition that includes that term or something close to it and doesn't explain it independently.

circumstance, causal Sometimes spoken of as a sufficient condition for something else. A set of conditions, usually with one of them taken as the cause of the effect, and prior to it in time. Circumstance and effect are in lawful or whatever-else connection. *See also* lawful connection.

cognitive consciousness Kinds of thinking as against kinds of wanting with affective consciousness. Representations, including sentences, having to do with truth. *Cf.* affective consciousness. *Go to* the summary table, pp. 162–3.

cognitive science The science of consciousness and also unconscious mentality.

conditional statement A fundamental kind of if-then statement, of the form *if x occurs then, whatever else occurs with it, y also occurs* – or an if-then statement based on a fundamental one.

conscious representations *See* representations, conscious.

consciousness Ordinary consciousness in the primary or core sense given in a good dictionary, such as *The New Oxford Dictionary of English*.

consciousness, three sides of *See* three sides.

consensus Informed general or pretty general agreement about something, as in science, sometimes written into accounts of scientific method.

content of conscious state or event In some views contrasted with the rest of the conscious state or event, maybe called the vehicle of the content. Could also be used, but has not been, in the sense of including subjective physical worlds with perceptual consciousness and representations with cognitive and affective consciousness.

criteria for an adequate theory or analysis of consciousness For a good theory of consciousness we need to see and assemble what criteria of adequacy it will have to satisfy, the tests it has to pass. These include distinctions of three sides of consciousness, its difference, its reality, answer to what is actual, answer to what actuality is, naturalist account, accounts of relations and subjectivity.

database, actual consciousness Our concepts for, our thinking about, the results of our holds on, our consciousness in the primary ordinary sense, summed up as something being actual, named actual consciousness and subsequently analysed as subjective physicality of three kinds, those in perceptual consciousness, cognitive consciousness and affective consciousness. *See also* actual consciousness as initally clarified.

dependency relations Lawful relations between things, in particular both of physical worlds and represenations. *See* lawful connections.

determinism Views to the effect that all events or occurrences, and in particular all our choices and decisions, are effects – necessary results of causal circumstances and sequences of them, everything in them also being effects. *See also* circumstance, causal, causal connection. *Cf.* origination.

direct realism *See* naive realism.

dispositional belief To have a dispositional belief now is for it to be the case only that some stimulus, maybe a question, *would* issue in a conscious belief somehow understood, maybe an actual belief.

dualism The traditional theory that mind and brain are two things, not one, usually the theory that conscious states and events are not one thing with physical states and events.

eliminative materialism Originally seemingly to the effect that it will turn out in a future neuroscience that there simply aren't any beliefs or desires as all we folk know them, just other categories instead.

empiricism, first-person Attention to one's holds on one's consciousness.

epiphenomenalism The views that conscious states and events do not cause behaviour and its effects, despite being in some connection with brain states and events that do cause behaviour and its effects.

evolutionary causalism The idea that Representations are things somehow caused by what they represent, but of more survival-value for us, more biological advantage, more evolutionary advantage, than certain other conceivable representations.

experience, experiencing Usually used for consciousness, being conscious, in the primary ordinary sense. Used primarily with perceptual consciousness.

explanationism *See* determinism.

externalism Views to the effect that conscious states and events, rather than only being about external facts, somehow consist in such facts.

freedom Commonly understood as being of two kinds, voluntariness and origination. *See* voluntariness, origination, determinism.

functionalism, abstract The view that conscious states and events are to be understood in terms of their relations to their causes and effects, and are in some connection or correlation with physical states and events but are themselves abstract or non-physical.

functionalism, physical The view that conscious states and events are physical events to be understood partly in terms of their relations to their causes and effects. *See also* functionalism, abstract.

hallucination, argument from The argument that perception is a matter of representations such as sense-data since perception is fundamentally like hallucination and hallucination is a matter only of representations. *Cf.* naive realism.

higher-order states For John Searle, conscious states are biological, but *higher-order* states than others – each higher state is realized in and also caused by lower-level neural or neurobiological elements in the brain. Like higher-level states of liquidity of water as against the molecules, and so on.

higher-order thought (HOT) theory For David Rosenthal and Peter Carruthers, conscious states are conscious in the sense that we have not only them but states about them, an awareness or thought of them – a higher-order thought.

hold on your consciousness What issues in your now being able to recall and at least to some extent characterize a recent conscious event, say the one owed to reading the words 'hold on your own consciousness' – or an event of perceptual or affective consciousness.

idealism The philosophical term is oddly used as a name for the doctrines of what you can call philosophers of spirit, including Hegel, in the confrontatation between them and materialists.

ideas, leading, about consciousness *See* leading ideas of consciousness.

identity theory, mind–brain The theory that conscious events and states are numerically identical with brain events and states. Thus typically a theory of objective physicalism.

illusion, argument from Argument that since we see a thing differently from different points of view and so on, we do not see a single external thing.

individuality The fundamental fact of the subjectivity of consciousness, an understanding in terms of a unity of a conscious thing akin to personal identity rightly conceived.

intentionality Old but misleading use of the word by some philosophers for aboutness, the character or fact of something that is its being about or of, or its representing, something else.

introspection Inner seeing, not to be identified with only your hold on your own consciousness.

language of thought (LOT) A language supposed by Ned Block to be fundamental to or inherent in all consciousness, whatever natural languages may be involved in it.

lawful connections Connections between states or events, which connections are or are related to fundamental ones – which are such that if or since one thing occurs, typically a set of necessary conditions, then, whatever else is happening, the other thing occurs. *See also* circumstance, causal.

leading ideas of consciousness Consciousness as a matter of (i) qualia, (ii) what it is like to be something, (iii) traditional subjectivity or a self, (iv) aboutness or intentionality, (v) phenomenality.

lingualism General philosophy of language applied to philosophy of mind.

locations of consciousness With perceptual consciousness, both external and internal to the perceiver. With cognitive and affective consciousness, internal.

logic of ordinary intelligence Concern for (i) clarity, usually in the form of analysis, (ii) consistency and validity, (iii) completness, (iv) generalness.

mental images Conscious representations resembling such ordinary images as photos and portraits.

mentalism Conception of consciousness as including, in terms of other conceptions of consciousness, both conscious and unconscious mental events and states, for example, conscious and unconscious in terms of actual consciousness.

mentality Conscious and unconscious states and events that are explanatory of at least behaviour, the unconscious states and events somehow related to consciousness, so as to exclude mere musculature and so on.

metaphysics Sometimes used for or with reference only to the general question of this book, the general nature of consciousness, and hence the various theories of it. For entirely more general usages, here and elsewhere, see the several entries in *The Oxford Companion to Philosophy*. *Cf.* the entries on philosophy.

mind, the mind Often used loosely, in effect for either consciousness or consciousness plus other mentality.

mind–body problem The problem of the relation of the mind to the brain. In fact the relation of perceptual, cognitive and affective consciousness as analysed to the brain. In Actualism ordinary lawful connection.

multiple realizability The idea that, for example, we and chimps and snakes and conceivably computers can be in exactly the very same pain or other conscious state but it goes with or is realized in quite different physical states. *See also* functionalism.

mysterianism The belief or attitude that consciousness will remain a mystery to us. An extreme statement of it is that we have no more chance of getting to the nature of consciousness than chimps have of doing quantum physics.

naive realism The conviction that perception is not a matter of a relation of the perceiver to an inner sense datum or other representation, but rather some direct relation to the thing perceived.

naturalism Restriction to consideration of things and states of affairs wholly open in principle to understanding by way of the scientific method.

neutral monism The theory that Objective physical things and conscious things are in fact two different organizations of a single stuff.

nomic connection *See* lawful connection.

origination Freedom that is free will with respect to choices and actions, this being initiation of them that is uncaused, not an effect, and yet something for which a person is responsible. *Cf.* voluntariness.

panpsychism The doctrine usually spoken of as being that *mind* is an inner feature of anything and everything.

perception Process of seeing, hearing, touching and so on, of which perceptual consciousness is evidently a part rather than the whole.

perceptual consciousness Consciousness in perception, as against cognitive and affective consciousness. *Go to* the summary table, pp. 162–3.

phenomenality Spoken of as the character or nature of experiencing, contrasted with access consciousness or dispositional mentality.

philosophy Greater concentration than that of science on the logic of ordinary intelligence, this consisting in clarity, consistency and validity, generalness, and completeness. *See also* scientific method.

philosophy and science *See* philosophy.

physical That which consists in the two species objective physicality and subjective physicalities, the latter being the three sides of consciousness.

physical, objective By having specified characteristics, some shared with subjective physicality, some not. *Go to* the summary table, pp. 162–3.

physical, subjective By having characteristics some of which are different from those of the objective physical world. *Go to* the summary table, pp. 162–3.

physical, subjective world *See* subjective physical worlds.

physicality, characteristics of *See* characteristics of physicality.

physicalism Almost always understood as theories of consciousness being physical in the objective or devout scientific sense – the mind is just the brain.

privacy In a special sense, what is private is what is open to privileged access. *See* privileged access.

privileged access Owed to a greater confidence than others can have about one's own conscious states and events, certainly not infallibility.

qualia Items in or of consciousness variously described. Including ways things seem, features of mental states, experiential properties of sensations or feelings, perceptions, wants and emotions, or somehow similar properties of thinking itself somehow conceived.

questions, main, about consciousness The different natures of the three sides of consciousness, the general or shared nature of all consciousness. Also the mind–body problem and so on.

radical externalism *See* externalism.

real Term so variously used as to resist summary. Sometimes for: somehow physical (as primarily in this book), existing, actual, true nature of, experienced, what something else is reducible to, fundamental, essential.

relationism or **computerism** The foremost form of physical functionism.

realizability *See* multiple realizability.

representations Things about other things, aboutnesses.

representations, conscious Representations with the further property of being actual in the sense of being in a particular way subjectively physical – in dependency relations with other mental events and commonly with subjective physical worlds.

representations, their actuality *See* representations, conscious.

right subject re: consciousness A most defensible adequate initial clarification of consciousness.

room, a Used typically in this book as an example of a stage of a subjective physical world.

room, subjectively physical Familiar kind of phase or whatever of a subjective physical world.

science-factual inquiry According to scientific method, distinguished from philosophy by a lesser concentration on the logic of ordinary intelligence.

scientific method Method of inquiry commonly based on empirical or measurable or experimental evidence subject to specific principles of reasoning. *See also* philosophy.

self, traditional Inner entity, subject, special personal unity not consisting in related things, metaphysical entity, homunculus, taken as basic fact of subjectivity with respect to consciousness. *See also* subjectivity, unity, individuality.

stage Space-time part of a subjective physical world.

state of affairs or circumstance A thing or things having properties and/or relations.

subjective physical worlds All that is and has been actual with respect to the perceptual consciousness of a particular perceiver.

subjective physical worlds, their actuality The subjective physicality of these worlds, their relations of dependency with the objective physical world and with a perceiver neurally. *Cf.* representations, conscious.

subjectivity Fundamentally a general fact of consciousness. Also used in opposition to objectivity. In Actualism subjectivity or consciousness is initially clarified by way of a database and fundamentally analysed in terms of subjective physical worlds and subjective physical representations.

Summary Table of Physicalities Includes four categories of physical things: the genus of physical things in general, the species objective physical worlds, the species subjective physical worlds, the species subjective physical representations.

supervenience Dependency relation of an event or state of consciousness somehow conceived to a brain state or other physical state. *See also* mind–body problem.

table of physicalities *See* Summary Table of Physicalities.

theory or **analysis of consciousness** Account of the nature of consciousness, what it is, preferably the result, for a start, of an adequate initial clarification of consciousness, perhaps as actual consciousness. *Cf.* clarification, adequate initial.

Theory of Descriptions, Russell's At the very bottom, the proposition used to save the idea that meanings are things referred, which faces the objection that terms referring to nothing can be meaningful, that such terms are certain descriptions.

three sides of consciousness Perceptual, cognitive and affective. *See also* subjective physical worlds, representations.

union theory Honderich theory of consciousness and mind in *A Theory of Determinism: The Mind, Neuroscience, and Life-hopes* and *How Free Are You?*, wholly superseded by Actualism.

unity The unity involved in an ongoing consciousness, misconceived as a traditional self, rightly conceived as a unity united by dependencies and interdependencies of lawfulness and meaning. It is a unity consisting in perceptual, cognitive and affective consciouness and more of the mental than that.

voluntariness Freedom in choices and actions that is being uncompelled or unconstrained or a matter of embraced desires. Consistent with determinism. *Cf.* origination.

zombies Conceivable things, typically objectively physical things, like humans, which according to certain theories or analyses of consciousness are conscious, but are not conscious in the primary ordinary or core sense or something like it.

READINGS ON CONCIOUSNESS

General or Inclusive

Bennett, Jonathan, *Locke, Berkeley, Hume: Central Themes* (Oxford, 1999)

Blakemore, Susan, *Consciousness: An Introduction* (Oxford, 2004)

Block, Ned, Owen Flanagan and Guven Guzeldere, eds, *The Nature of Consciousness: Philosophical Debates* (Cambridge, MA, 1997)

—, ed., *Philosophy of Mind: Classical and Contemporary Readings* (Oxford, 2002)

—, ed., *Readings in Philosophy of Psychology* (London, 1980)

Brown, Harold, 'Comment on Radical Externalism', in *Radical Externalism: Honderich's Theory of Consciousness Discussed*, ed. Anthony Freeman (Exeter, 2006)

Burge, Tyler, *Foundations of Mind* (Oxford, 2007)

Campbell, Neil, *A Brief Introduction to the Philosophy of Mind* (Peterborough, 2005)

Critchley, Simon, *Continental Philosophy: A Very Short Introduction* (Chicago, IL, 2001)

Caruso, Gregg, ed., *Ted Honderich on Consciousness, Determinism and Humanity* (forthcoming, 2018). Papers after a University of London day of lectures on all of Honderich's philosophy: philosophy of mind, moral and political philosophy, determinism/explanationism and freedom. Papers by Noam Chomsky, Paul Snowdon, Barbara Gail Montero, Michael Neumann, Barry Smith, Gregg Caruso, Derk Pereboom, Saul Smilansky, Paul Gilbert, Mary Warnock, Alastair Hannay, Kevin Timpe, Richard Norman. Replies by Ted Honderich.

Chalmers, David, *The Conscious Mind: In Search of a Fundamental Theory* (Oxford, 1996)

Chomsky, Noam, 'Replies', in *Chomsky and His Critics*, ed. Louise Antony and Norbert Hornstein (Oxford, 2003)

Cockburn, David, *An Introduction to the Philosophy of Mind* (Basingstoke, 2001)

Crane, Tim, 'Comment on Ted Honderich's Radical Externalism', in *Radical Externalism: Honderich's Theory of Consciousness Discussed*, ed. Anthony Freeman (Exeter, 2006)

—, *Elements of Mind: An Introduction to Philosophy of Mind* (Oxford, 2002)

Dennett, Daniel, *Consciousness Explained* (London, 1991)

—, *The Intentional Stance* (Cambridge, MA, 1987)

Fodor, Jerry, *Psychological Explanation: An Introduction to the Philosophy of Psychology* (New York, 1968)

Freeman, Anthony, ed., *Radical Externalism: Honderich's Theory of Consciousness Discussed* (Exeter, 2006). Papers by Harold Brown, Tim Crane, James Garvey, Stephen Law, E. J. Lowe, Derek Matravers, Paul Noordhof, Ingmar Persson, Stephen Priest, Barry C. Smith, Paul Snowdon. Brief replies by Ted Honderich.

Garvey, James, 'Consciousness and Absence', in *Radical Externalism: Honderich's Theory of Consciousness Discussed*, ed. Anthony Freeman (Exeter, 2006)

Gray, Jeffrey, *Consciousness: Creeping Up on the Hard Problem* (Oxford, 2004)

Gregory, Richard, ed., *The Oxford Companion to the Mind* (Oxford, 2004)

Grim, Patrick, ed., *Mind and Consciousness: Five Questions* (Exeter, 2009)

Guttenplan, Samuel, ed., *A Companion to the Philosophy of Mind* (Oxford, 1994)

Hannay, Alastair, *Human Consciousness* (London, 1990)

—, review discussion of *Actual Consciousness*, *Philosophy*, XC/352 (2015), pp. 317–28

Heil, John, *Philosophy of Mind: A Contemporary Introduction* (London, 1998)

—, ed., *Philosophy of Mind: A Guide and Anthology* (Oxford, 2004)

Honderich, Ted, *On Consciousness*, collected papers (Edinburgh, 2004)

—, ed., *The Oxford Companion to Philosophy* – many entries on consciousness and mind (Oxford, 2005)

—, ed., *Philosophers of Our Times: Royal Institute of Philosophy Annual Lectures* (Oxford, 2015)

—, 'Radical Externalism', introduction to *Radical Externalism: Honderich's Theory of Consciousness Discussed*, ed. Anthony Freeman (Exeter, 2006)

—, Website; many relevant papers, lectures etc. www.homepages.ucl. ac.uk/~uctytho

Jacquette, Dale, review discussion of *Actual Consciousness* (*Notre Dame Philosophical Reviews*, 2015)

Kim, Jaegwon, *Philosophy of Mind* (Boulder, CO, 1998)

Law, Stephen, 'Honderich and the Curse of Epiphenomenalism', in *Radical Externalism: Honderich's Theory of Consciousness Discussed*, ed. Anthony Freeman (Exeter, 2006)

Lowe, E. J., *An Introduction to the Philosophy of Mind* (Cambridge, 2000)

—, 'Radical Externalism or Berkeley Revisited?', in *Radical Externalism: Honderich's Theory of Consciousness Discussed*, ed. Anthony Freeman (Exeter, 2006)

Lycan, William, *Consciousness* (Cambridge, MA, 1987)

—, *Consciousness and Experience* (Cambridge, MA, 1996)

McGinn, Colin, *Consciousness and Its Objects* (Oxford, 2004)

—, *The Mysterious Flame: Conscious Minds in a Material World* (New York, 1999)

—, *The Problem of Consciousness: Essays Towards a Resolution* (Oxford, 1991)

McLaughlin, Brian, Ansgar Beckermann and Sven Walter, eds, *The Oxford Handbook of Philosophy of Mind* (Oxford, 2009)

Margolis, Eric, Richard Samuels and Stephen Stich, eds, *The Oxford Handbook of Philosophy of Cognitive Science* (Oxford, 2012)

Matravers, Derek, 'Some Questions about Radical Externalism', in *Radical Externalism: Honderich's Theory of Consciousness Discussed*, ed. Anthony Freeman (Exeter, 2006)

Metzinger, Thomas, *Conscious Experience* (Upton Pyne, Devon, 1995)

Noordhof, Paul, 'The Success of Consciousness', in *Radical Externalism: Honderich's Theory of Consciousness Discussed*, ed. Anthony Freeman (Exeter, 2006)

O'Hear, Anthony, ed., *Current Issues in the Philosophy of Mind* (Cambridge, 1998)

Papineau, David, *Philosophical Naturalism* (Oxford, 1993)

—, *Thinking about Consciousness* (Oxford, 2002)

Persson, Ingmar, 'Consciousness as Existence as a Form of Neutral Monism', in *Radical Externalism: Honderich's Theory of Consciousness Discussed*, ed. Anthony Freeman (Exeter, 2006)

Priest, Stephen, 'Radical Internalism', in *Radical Externalism: Honderich's Theory of Consciousness Discussed*, ed. Anthony Freeman (Exeter, 2006)

—, *Theories of the Mind* (London, 1991)

Ravenscroft, Ian, *Philosophy of Mind: A Beginner's Guide* (Oxford, 2005)

Robinson, Daniel, ed., *The Mind* (Oxford, 1998)

Seager, William, *Theories of Consciousness: An Introduction and Assessment* (London, 1999)

Searle, John, *Consciousness and Language* (Cambridge, 2002)

—, *Intentionality: An Essay in the Philosophy of Mind* (Cambridge, 1983)

—, *Mind: A Brief Introduction* (Oxford, 2004)

—, *The Mystery of Consciousness* (New York, 1999)

—, *The Rediscovery of the Mind* (Cambridge, MA, 1992)

Smith, Barry, 'Consciousness: An Inner View of the Outer World', in *Radical Externalism: Honderich's Theory of Consciousness Discussed*, ed. Anthony Freeman (Exeter, 2006)

Smith, Quentin, and Aleksandar Jokic, eds, *Consciousness: New Philosophical Perspectives* (Oxford, 2003)

Snowdon, Paul, 'Radical Externalisms', in *Radical Externalism: Honderich's Theory of Consciousness Discussed*, ed. Anthony Freeman (Exeter, 2006)

Strawson, Galen, *Mental Reality* (Cambridge, MA, 1994)

Sturgeon, Scott, *Matters of Mind: Consciousness, Reason and Nature* (London, 2000)

Tye, Michael, *Consciousness Revisited* (Cambridge, MA, 2009)

—, *The Metaphysics of Mind* (Cambridge, 1998)
—, *Ten Problems of Consciousness* (Cambridge, MA, 1995)
Velmans, Max, *Understanding Consciousness* (London, 2009)
—, and Susan Schneider, eds, *The Blackwell Companion to Consciousness*
    (Oxford, 2007)

Readings by Chapter

1 Actualism Anticipated

Ayer, A. J., *The Central Questions of Philosophy* (London, 1976)
Block, Ned, *Consciousness, Function, and Representation, Collected Papers*, vol. I
    (Cambridge, MA, 2007)
Burge, Tyler, *Foundations of Mind* (Oxford, 2007)
Chalmers, David, *The Conscious Mind: In Search of a Fundamental Theory*
    (Oxford, 1996)
Chomsky, Noam, 'Replies', in *Chomsky and His Critics*, ed. Louise Antony and
    Norbert Hornstein (Oxford, 2003)
Clark, Andy, *Being There: Putting Brain, Body and World Together Again*
    (Cambridge, MA, 1997)
Crane, Tim, *The Elements of Mind* (Oxford, 2001)
—, 'Intentionality as the Mark of the Mental', in *Current Issues in the Philosophy*
    of Mind, ed. Anthony O'Hear (Cambridge, 1998)
—, *The Mechanical Mind* (London, 1995)
—, *The Objects of Thought* (Oxford, 2013)
Dennett, Daniel, 'Quining Qualia', in *The Nature of Consciousness: Philosophical*
    Debates, ed. Ned Block, Owen Flanagan and Guven Guzeldere (Cambridge,
    MA, 1997)
Fodor, Jerry, *Psychosemantics: The Problem of Meaning in the Philosophy of Mind*
    (Cambridge, MA, 1987)
Honderich, Ted, *How Free Are You? The Determinism Question* (Oxford, 2002)
—, *A Theory of Determinism: The Mind, Neuroscience, and Life-hopes* (Oxford,
    1988)
Nagel, Thomas, 'Conceiving the Impossible and the Mind–body Problem', in
    Honderich, *Philosophers of Our Times* (Oxford, 2015)
—, 'What is It Like to Be a Bat?', in *Philosophical Review*, LXXXIII/4 (1974) and
    reprinted in *Mortal Questions* (Oxford, 1979)
Noë, Alva, *Out of Our Heads: Why You Are Not Your Brain, and Other Lessons*
    from the Biology of Consciousness (New York, 2009)
Schrift, Alan D., ed., book series: *The History of Continental Philosophy*
    (Chicago, IL, 2010)
Searle, John, *Mind: A Brief Introduction* (Oxford, 2004)
—, *The Rediscovery of the Mind* (Cambridge, MA, 1992)

2 Four Main Questions About Consciousness

Block, Ned, *Consciousness, Function and Representation: Collected Papers* (Cambridge, MA, 2007)

Chalmers, David, *The Conscious Mind: In Search of a Fundamental Theory* (Oxford, 1996)

Chomsky, Noam, 'Replies', in *Chomsky and His Critics*, ed. Louise Antony and Norbert Hornstein (Oxford, 2003)

Dennett, Daniel, *Consciousness Explained* (London, 1991)

Fodor, Jerry, 'Meaning and the World Order', in *The Problem of Meaning in the Philosophy of Mind* (Cambridge, MA, 1987)

Garvey, James, 'What Does McGinn Think We Cannot Know?', *Analysis*, LVII/3 (1997)

Greenfield, Susan, *The Private Life of the Brain* (London, 2000)

Honderich, Ted, *Actual Consciousness* (Oxford, 2014)

—, *Right and Wrong, and Palestine, 9–11, Iraq, 7–7 . . .* (New York, 2006) Also titled *Humanity, Terrorism, Terrorist War: Palestine, 9/11, Iraq, 7/7 . . .* (London, 2006)

Hume, David, *Abstract* (Cambridge, 1958)

—, *Enquiries* (Oxford, 1962)

—, *A Treatise of Human Nature* (Oxford, 1958)

McGinn, Colin, 'Can We Solve the Mind–body Problem?', in McGinn, *The Problem of Consciousness: Essays Towards a Resolution* (Oxford, 1991)

—, *The Problem of Consciousness: Essays Towards a Resolution* (Oxford, 1991)

Nagel, Thomas, 'What is It Like to Be a Bat?', in *Mortal Questions* (Oxford, 1979)

Popper, Karl, and J. C. Eccles, *The Self and Its Brain* (Berlin, 1987)

Searle, John, *The Rediscovery of the Mind* (New Haven, CT, 1992)

Wittgenstein, Ludwig, *Zettel* (Berkeley, CA, 1967)

—, *Remarks on the Philosophy of Psychology* (Oxford, 1980)

3 Five Leading Ideas About Consciousness

Ayer, A. J., *The Central Questions of Philosophy* (London, 1976)

—, *The Problem of Knowledge* (London, 1956)

Bennett, Jonathan, *Locke, Berkeley, Hume: Central Themes* (Oxford, 1999)

Block, Ned, 'On a Confusion about a Function of Consciousness', in *Consciousness, Function and Representation: Collected Papers* (Cambridge, MA, 2007)

Chalmers, David, *The Conscious Mind: In Search of a Fundamental Theory* (Oxford, 1996)

Crane, Tim, *The Elements of Mind* (Oxford, 2001)

—, 'Intentionality as the Mark of the Mental', in *Current Issues in the Philosophy of Mind*, ed. Anthony O'Hear (Cambridge, 1998)

—, *The Mechanical Mind* (London, 1995)

—, *The Objects of Thought* (Oxford, 2013)

Dennett, Daniel, *Consciousness Explained* (London, 1991)

—, 'Quining Qualia', in *The Nature of Consciousness: Philosophical Debates*, ed. Ned Block, Owen Flanagan and Guzen Guzeldere (Cambridge, MA, 1997)

Hamlyn, David, *Being a Philosopher: The History of a Practice* (London, 1993)

Martin, Mike, 'Setting Things Before the Mind', in *Current Issues in the Philosophy of Mind*, ed. A. O'Hear (Cambridge, 1998)

Mole, Christopher, Declan Smythies and Wayne Wu, eds, *Attention: Philosophical and Psychological Essays* (Oxford, 2011)

Nagel, Thomas, 'Conceiving the Impossible and the Mind–body Problem', in *Philosophers of Our Times*, ed. Ted Honderich (Oxford, 2015)

—, 'What Is it Like to Be a Bat?', in *Mortal Questions* (Oxford, 1979)

Peacocke, Chris, *Sense and Content: Experience, Thought and Their Relations* (Oxford, 1983)

Russell, Bertrand, *The Problems of Philosophy* (Oxford, 1912)

Searle, John, *Consciousness and Language* (Cambridge, 2002)

Sprigge, Timothy, *The Vindication of Absolute Idealism* (Edinburgh, 1984)

Wilson, Margaret Dauler, *Descartes* (London, 1978)

Williams, Bernard, 'Philosophy as a Humanistic Discipline', in *Philosophers of Our Times*, ed. Ted Honderich (Oxford, 2015)

4 A Database

Baars, Bernard, *In the Theatre of the Consciousness: The Workspace of the Mind* (Oxford, 1997)

Beckermann, Ansgar, and Sven Walter, eds, *The Oxford Handbook of Philosophy of Mind* (Oxford, 2009)

Chalmers, David, 'Why Isn't There More Progress in Philosophy?', in *Philosophers of Our Times*, ed. Ted Honderich (Oxford, 2015)

Feigl, Herbert, *The Mental and the Physical* (Minneapolis, MN, 1967)

Jackson, Frank, *Mind, Method, and Conditionals: Selected Essays* (London, 1986)

—, 'What Mary Didn't Know', *Journal of Philosophy*, LXXXIII/5 (1986)

James, William, *Psychology* (Cleveland, OH, 1892)

McGinn, Colin, 'Can We Solve the Mind–body Problem?' in *The Problem of Consciousness: Essays Towards a Resolution* (Oxford, 1989)

Montero, Barbara, 'What is Physical?', in *The Oxford Handbook of Philosophy of Mind*, ed. Brian McLaughlin and Ansgar Sven Walter (Oxford, 2009)

Peacocke, Christopher, *Sense and Content: Experience, Thought, and Their Relations* (Oxford, 1983)

—, *Thoughts: An Essay on Content* (Oxford, 1986)

Schwitzgebel, Eric, 'Introspection', *The Stanford Encyclopedia of Philosophy*, ed. Edward N. Zalta, available at https://plato.stanford.edu/archives

5 Mind–Brain Dualism, Abstract Functionalism

Block, Ned, 'On a Confusion about a Function of Consciousness', in *The Nature of Consciousness: Philosophical Debates*, ed. Block, Owen Flanagan and Guzen Guzeldere (Cambridge, MA, 1987)

Chalmers, David, *The Conscious Mind: In Search of a Fundamental Theory* (Oxford, 1996)

Chomsky, Noam, review of B. F. Skinner book *Verbal Behavior*, *Language*, XXXV/1 (1959)

Eccles, J. C., and Karl Popper, *The Self and Its Brain* (Berlin, 1977)

Honderich, Ted, *On Consciousness*, collected papers (Edinburgh, 2004)

James, William, *Psychology* (Cleveland, OH, 1892)

Robinson, Howard, *Objections to Physicalism* (Oxford, 1993)

6 Other Particular Consciousness Theories

Burge, Tyler, *Foundations of Mind* (Oxford, 2007)

Carruthers, Peter, *Language, Thought and Consciousness: An Essay in Philosophical Psychology* (Cambridge, 1996)

Chalmers, David, *The Conscious Mind: In Search of a Fundamental Theory* (Oxford, 1996)

Churchland, Patricia, *Neurophilosophy* (Cambridge, MA, 1986)

Churchland, Paul, *Matter and Consciousness* (Cambridge, MA, 1988)

Clark, Andy, *Being There: Putting Brain, Body and World Together Again* (Cambridge, MA, 1997)

Davidson, Donald, *Essays on Actions and Events* (Oxford, 1980)

Dennett, Daniel, *Consciousness Explained* (London, 1991)

Hameroff, Stuart, 'Consciousness, Neurobiology and Quantum Mechanics', in *The Emerging Physics of Consciousness*, ed. Jack A. Tuszynski (Berlin, 2006)

Hannay, Alastair, *Human Consciousness* (London, 1990)

Honderich, Ted, 'The Champion of Mauve', *Analysis*, XLIV/2 (1984), pp. 86–9. Reprinted with other relevant papers in Neil Campbell, *Mental Causation and the Metaphysics of Mind* (Peterborough, 2003)

—, *A Theory of Determinism: The Mind, Neuroscience and Life-hopes* (Oxford, 1988). Republished as *Mind and Brain* and *The Consequences of Determinism*

Kim, Jaegwon, *Physicalism, Or Something Near Enough* (Princeton, NJ, 2005)

Noë, Alva, *Out of Our Heads: Why You are Not Your Brain, and Other Lessons from the Biology of Consciousness* (New York, 2009)

Papineau, David, *Philosophical Naturalism* (Oxford, 1993)

Persson, Ingmar, *The Primacy of Perception: Towards a Neutral Monism* (Gleerup, 1985)

Priest, Stephen, 'Radical Internalism', in *Radical Externalism: Honderich's Theory of Consciousness Discussed*, ed. Anthony Freeman (Exeter, 2006)

Putnam, Hilary, *Mental Reality* (Cambridge, MA, 1994)
—, *Mind, Language and Reality: Philosophical Papers*, vol. II (Cambridge, 1975)
Pylkkanen, Paavo, *Mind, Matter and the Implicate Order* (Berlin, 2007)
Rosenthal, David, *Consciousness and Mind* (Oxford, 2005)
Russell, Bertrand, *The Analysis of Mind* (London, 1921)
Searle, John, *Mental Reality* (Cambridge, MA, 2009)
—, *Speech Acts: An Essay in the Philosophy of Mind* (Cambridge, 1969)
—, *The Rediscovery of the Mind* (Cambridge, MA, 1992)
Strawson, Galen, *Real Materialism and Other Essays* (Oxford, 2008)

7 The Characteristics of the Chair Under You

Ayers, Michael, *Locke* (London, 1991)
Beckermann, Sven Walter, eds, *The Oxford Handbook of Philosophy of Mind* (Oxford, 2009)
Chomsky, Noam, 'Replies to Lycan, Poland, Strawson et al.', in *Chomsky and His Critics*, ed. Louise Antony and Norbert Hornstein (Oxford, 2003)
Crane, Tim, and D. H. Mellor, 'There is No Question of Physicalism', *Mind*, XCIX/394 (1990)
Feigl, Herbert, *The Mental and the Physical: The Essay and a Postscript* (Minneapolis, MN, 1967)
Honderich, Ted, *How Free Are You?* (Oxford, 2002)
—, 'Temporal Relations and Temporal Qualities', in *Time and Philosophy*, ed. Paul Ricoeur (Paris, 1977)
—, *A Theory of Determinism: The Mind, Neuroscience, and Life-hopes* (Oxford, 1998)
Lycan, William, 'The Mind–body Problem', in *The Oxford Handbook of Philosophy of Cognitive Science*, ed. Eric Margolis, Richard Samuels and Stephen Stich (Oxford, 2012)
Montero, Barbara, 'What is Physical?', in *The Oxford Handbook of Philosophy of Mind*, ed. Brian McLaughlin, Ansgar Beckermann and Sven Walter (Oxford, 2009)
Sosa, E., 'Privileged Access', in *Consciousness*, ed. Quentin Smith and Aleksandar Jokic (Oxford, 2003)
Stoljar, Daniel, *Ignorance and Imagination: The Epistemic Origin of the Problem of Consciousness* (Oxford, 2006)
Stich, Stephen, ed., *Mental Representation: A Reader* (Oxford, 1994)

8 Consciousness in Seeing: What Is Actual?

Ayer, A. J., *The Central Questions of Philosophy* (London, 1976)
—, *The Problem of Knowledge* (London, 1956)

Baars, Bernard J., *In the Theatre of Consciousness: The Workspace of the Mind* (New York, 1997)

Block, Ned, 'Attention and Mental Paint', in *Philosophers of Our Times*, ed. Ted Honderich (Oxford, 2015)

—, 'Mental Paint', in *Consciousness, Function and Representation: Collected Papers* (Cambridge, MA, 2007)

Burge, Tyler, *Origins of Objectivity* (Oxford, 2010)

Coates, Paul, *The Metaphysics of Perception: Wilfrid Sellars, Perceptual Consciousness and Critical Realism* (London, 2007)

Crane, Tim, 'Comment on Radical Externalism', in *Radical Externalism: Honderich's Theory of Consciousness Discussed*, ed. Anthony Freeman (Exeter, 2006)

Critchley, Simon, *Continental Philosophy: A Very Short Introduction* (Chicago, IL, 2001)

Fodor, Jerry, 'The Revenge of the Given: Mental Representation', in *Philosophers of Our Times*, ed. Ted Honderich (Oxford, 2015)

Freeman, Anthony, ed., *Radical Externalism: Honderich's Theory of Consciousness Discussed* (Exeter, 2006). Papers by Harold Brown, Tim Crane, James Garvey, Stephen Law, E. J. Lowe, Derek Matravers, Paul Noordhof, Ingmar Persson, Stephen Priest, Barry C. Smith, Paul Snowdon. Brief replies by Ted Honderich.

Gendler, Tamar Szabo, *Perceptual Experience* (Oxford, 2006)

The History of Continental Philosophy, book series edited by Alan D. Schrift (Chicago, 2010)

Honderich, Ted, 'Seeing Qualia and Positing the World', in *A. J. Ayer Memorial Essays*, ed. A. Phillips-Griffiths (Cambridge, 2011)

McGinn, Colin, *Consciousness and Its Objects* (Oxford, 2004)

MacIntyre, Alasdair, 'Social Structures and Their Threats to Moral Agency', in *Philosophers of Our Times*, ed. Ted Honderich (Oxford, 2015)

Martin, Michael, 'An Eye Directed Outward', in *Knowing Our Own Minds*, ed. Crispin Wright, Barry Smith and Cynthia Macdonald (Oxford, 1998)

Moore, G. E., *Philosophical Studies* (London, 1922)

Robinson, Howard, *Perception* (London, 1994)

Searle, John, *Intentionality: An Essay in the Philosophy of Mind* (Oxford, 1983)

Snowdon, Paul, 'The Formulation of Disjunctivism: A Response to Fish', *Proceedings of the Aristotelian Society*, CV (2005)

—, 'The Objects of Perceptual Experience', *Proceedings of the Aristotelian Society*, LXIV (1990)

Thompson, Janna, review of Honderich, *Actual Consciousness* in *Australian Book Review*, 390 (2015)

Valberg, J. J., *The Puzzle of Experience* (Oxford, 1992)

Strawson, Peter, 'Perception and Its Objects', in *Philosophers of Our Times*, ed. Ted Honderich (Oxford, 2015)

Warnock, G. J., *J. L. Austin* (London, 1989)

Wollheim, Richard, *On Drawing an Object*, inaugural lecture, University College London, 1964, in Wollheim, *On Art and the Mind* (Cambridge, MA, 1972)

9 Consciousness in Seeing: Being Actual

Crane, Tim, ed., *The Contents of Experience: Essays on Perception* (Cambridge, 1992)

Dretske, Fred, 'Representative Theory of Perception', in *The Oxford Companion to Philosophy*, ed. Ted Honderich (Oxford, 2005)

Freeman, Anthony, ed., *Radical Externalism: Honderich's Theory of Consciousness Discussed* (Exeter, 2006). Papers by Harold Brown, Tim Crane, James Garvey, Stephen Law, E. J. Lowe, Derek Matravers, Paul Noordhof, Ingmar Persson, Stephen Priest, Barry C. Smith, Paul Snowdon. Brief replies by Ted Honderich.

Grice, Paul, 'Method in Philosophical Psychology From the Banal to the Bizarre', *Proceedings and Addresses of the American Philosophical Association*, 48 (1975)

Kirk, Robert, *Zombies and Consciousness* (Oxford, 2005)

Lakatos, Imre, *The Methodology of Scientific Research Programmes* (Cambridge, 1978)

Martin, Michael, 'Beyond Dispute: Sense-data, Intentionality and the Mind–body Problem', in *History of the Mind–body Problem*, ed. Tim Crane and Sarah Patterson (London, 2000)

—, 'The Limits of Self-awareness', *Philosophical Studies*, CXX/1–3 (2004)

—, 'On Being Alienated', in *Perceptual Experience*, ed. T. S. Gendler and J. Hawthorne (Oxford, 2006)

—, 'Perception', in *The Oxford Handbook of Contemporary Philosophy*, ed. F. Jackson and M. Smith (Oxford, 2005)

—, 'The Transparency of Experience', *Mind and Language*, XVII/4 (2002)

Matravers, Derek, 'Some Questions about Radical Externalism', in *Radical Exteralism*, ed. Anthony Freeman (Exeter, 2006)

McGinn, Colin, 'Can We Solve the Mind–body Problem?', in *The Problem of Consciousness: Essays Towards a Resolution* (Oxford, 1989)

—, review of Honderich, *On Consciousness*, in *Philosophical Review*, 123 (2014). Review and replies on UCL homepage: hwww.homepages.ucl.ac.uk/~uctytho

Noë, Alva, *Action in Perception* (Cambridge, MA, 2006)

—, *Out of Our Heads* (Cambridge, MA, 2009)

Pitcher, George, *Berkeley* (London, 1977)

Strawson, Galen, *Mental Reality* (Cambridge, MA, 2009)

—, *Real Materialism and Other Essays* (Oxford, 2008)

Strawson, Peter, *Individuals: An Essay in Descriptive Metaphysics* (London, 1959)

van Inwagen, Peter, *Metaphysics* (Boulder, CO, 2008)

10 Thinking and Wanting: What Is Actual?

Bermúdez, José Luis, *Thinking Without Words* (Oxford, 2003)
Clapin, Hugh, ed., *Philosophy of Mental Representation* (Oxford, 2002)
Cummins, Robert, *The World in the Head* (Oxford, 2010)
Flanagan, Owen, *The Really Hard Problem: Meaning in a Material World* (Cambridge MA, 2007)
Fodor, Jerry, *The Language of Thought* (New York, 1975)
—, *LOT 2: The Language of Thought Revisited* (Cambridge, MA, 2008)
—, *Psychosemantics: The Problem of Meaning in the Philosophy of Mind* (Cambridge, MA, 1987)
Hannay, Alastair, *Mental Images: A Defence* (London, 1971)
Honderich, Ted, 'On Russell's Theory of Descriptions', *Proceedings of the Aristotelian Society*, New Series, LXIX (1969)
Honderich, *Right and Wrong, and Palestine, 9–11, Iraq, 7–7 . . .* (New York, 2006), also titled *Humanity, Terrorism, Terrorist War* (London, 2006)
Lycan, William G., *Mind and Cognition: A Reader* (Cambridge, MA, 1980)
Millikan, Ruth Garrett, *White Queen Psychology and Other Essays for Alice* (Cambridge, MA, 1993)
Papineau, David, *Reality and Representation* (Oxford, 1987)
Peacocke, Christopher, *Sense and Content: Experience, Thought, and Their Relations* (Oxford, 1983)
Searle, John, *Consciousness and Language* (Cambridge, 2002)
—, *Intentionality: An Essay in the Philosophy of Mind* (Cambridge, 1983)
—, *Speech Acts: An Essay in the Philosophy of Mind* (Cambridge, 1969)
—, 'Twenty-one Years in the Chinese Room', in *Views Into the Chinese Room: New Essays on Searle and Artificial Intelligence*, ed. J. Preston and M. Bishop (Oxford, 2002)
Sterelny, Kim, *The Representational Theory of Mind: An Introduction* (Oxford, 1990)
Woodfield, Andrew, ed., *Thought and Object: Essays on Intentionality* (Oxford, 1982)

11 Thinking and Wanting: Being Actual

Campbell, Neil, *Mental Causation and the Metaphysics of Mind: A Reader* (Peterborough, 2003)
Dennett, Daniel, *Consciousness Explained* (London, 1992)
Fodor, Jerry, *Psychosemantics: The Problem of Meaning in the Philosophy of Mind* (Cambridge, MA, 1987)
Honderich, Ted, *Actual Consciousness* (Oxford, 2014), Ch. 10
Nagel, Thomas, 'Conceiving the Impossible and the Mind–body Problem', in *Philosophers of Our Times*, ed. Ted Honderich (Oxford, 2015)

—, 'What is It Like to Be a Bat?', *Philosophical Review*, LXXXIII/4 (1974), reprinted in Nagel, *Mortal Questions* (Oxford, 1979)

Schneider, Susan, 'LOT, CTM, and the Elephant in the Room', *Synthese*, CLXX/2 (*2009*)

Searle, John, *Rationality in Action* (Cambridge, MA, 2001)

12 A Summary Table of Physicalities

Adler, Mortimer, *The Idea of Freedom: A Dialectical Examination of the Conceptions of Freedom* (New York, 1958)

Austin, J. L., *Sense and Sensibilia* (Oxford, 1962)

Ayer, A. J., *The Problem of Knowledge* (London, 1956)

Burge, Tyler, *Foundations of Mind* (Oxford, 2007)

Caruso, Gregg, ed., *Ted Honderich on Consciousness, Determinism and Humanity* (forthcoming, 2018). Papers after a University of London day of lectures on all of Honderich's philosophy: philosophy of mind, moral and political philosophy, determinism/explanationism and freedom. Papers by Noam Chomsky, Paul Snowdon, Barbara Gail Montero, Michael Neumann, Barry Smith, Gregg Caruso, Derk Pereboom, Paul Russell, Saul Smilansky, Paul Gilbert, Mary Warnock, Alastair Hannay, Kevin Timpe, Richard Norman. Replies by Ted Honderich.

Chalmers, David, *The Conscious Mind: In Search of a Fundamental Theory* (Oxford, 1996)

—, 'Why Isn't There More Progress in Philosophy?', in *Philosophers of Our Times*, ed. Ted Honderich (Oxford, 2015)

Chomsky, Noam, 'Replies to Lycan, Poland, Strawson et al.', in *Chomsky and His Critics*, ed. Louise Antony and Norbert Hornstein (Oxford, 2003)

Clark, Andy, *Being There: Putting Brain, Body and World Together Again* (Cambridge, MA, 1997)

Crane, Tim, *The Elements of Mind* (Oxford, 2001)

—, 'Intentionality as the Mark of the Mental', in *Current Issues in the Philosophy of Mind*, ed. Anthony O'Hear (Cambridge, 1998)

—, *The Mechanical Mind* (London, 1995)

—, *The Objects of Thought* (Oxford, 2013)

—, and Hugh Mellor, 'There is No Question of Physicalism', *Mind*, XCIX/394 (1990)

Fodor, Jerry, 'Meaning and the World Order', in *The Problem of Meaning in the Philosophy of Mind* (Cambridge, MA, 1987)

Hannay, Alastair, review discussion of Honderich, *Actual Consciousness*, *Philosophy*, 90 (2015)

Honderich, Ted, *Actual Consciousness* (Oxford, 2014), Ch. 11

—, *How Free Are You? The Determinism Problem* (Oxford, 2002)

—, *A Theory of Determinism: The Mind, Neuroscience, and Life-hopes* (Oxford, 1988)

—, lectures, papers and so on, University College London website:
www.homepages.ucl.ac.uk/uctytho

Kane, Robert, *The Oxford Handbook of Free Will* (Oxford, 1st edn 2002, 2nd edn 2011)

Kim, Jaegwon, *Physicalism, Or Something Near Enough* (Princeton, NJ, 2005)

Parfit, Derek, *Reasons and Persons* (Oxford, 1984)

—, 'We Are Not Human Beings', in *Philosophers of Our Times*, ed. Ted Honderich (Oxford, 2015)

Robinson, Howard, *Objections to Physicalism* (Oxford, 1993)

Rockwell, Teed, *Neither Brain Nor Ghost: A Nonindividualist Alternative to the Mind–brain Identity Theory* (Cambridge, MA, 2007)

Ryle, Gilbert, *The Concept of Mind* (Oxford, 1949)

Searle, John, *Consciousness and Language* (Cambridge, 2002)

—, 'Free Will as a Problem in Neurobiology', in *Philosophers of Our Times*, ed. Ted Honderich (Oxford, 2015)

Strawson, Galen, *Real Materialism and Other Essays* (Oxford, 2008)

—, *Selves: An Essay in Revisionary Metaphysics* (Oxford, 2009)

Strawson, Peter, 'Perception and Its Objects', in *Philosophers of Our Times*, ed. Ted Honderich (Oxford, 2016)

Wilson, Edgar, *The Mental as Physical* (London, 1979)

Wittgenstein, Ludwig, *Zettel* (Oakland, CA, 1967)

INDEX